Writings on Wade Guyton

JRP|RINGIER & LES PRESSES DU RÉEL

Tim Griffin [ed.]
Writings on Wade Guyton

Table of Contents

Introduction: Below The Fold
Tim Griffin

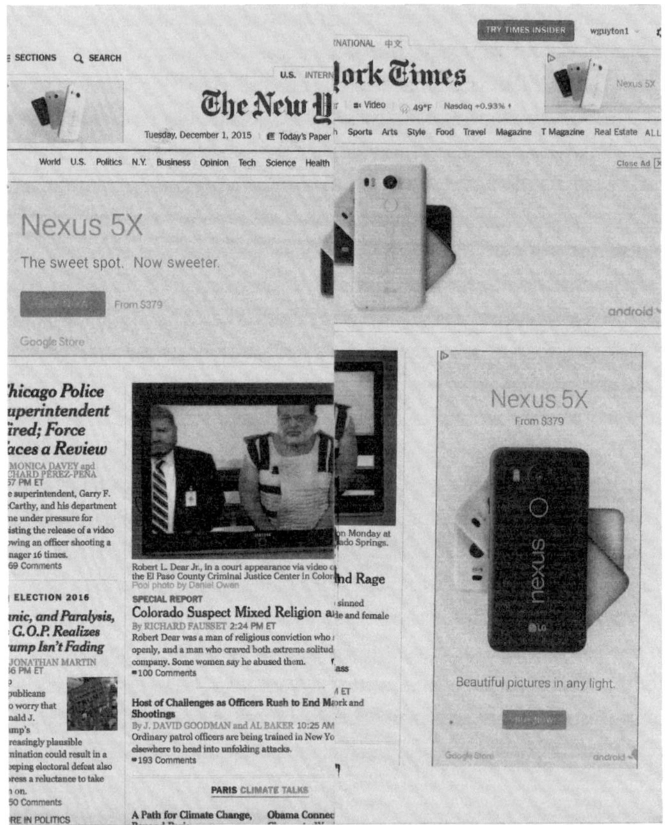

Untitled, 2015
Epson UltraChrome inkjet HDR on linen, 213.4 × 175.3 cm

From our perspective today, the year 2000—right around the time when Wade Guyton began appearing in exhibitions—seems at once incredibly distant and oddly prescient. Certainly, art-world dialogues that were happening then are apt to seem, if not the stuff of a lost history, over-determined. This dynamic is perhaps all the more ironic for the day's popular assertions that we were standing at the end of history, both in terms of technology's radical impact on our very experience of time and, just as important, with respect to the previous century's ideological paradigms having ostensibly run their course. Perhaps such a sense of internal contradiction makes any return to these discourses (whether around art, design, or networked culture) resonate all the more profoundly in the contemporary landscape: they provide so many bones within the social body we inhabit today. Yet if by this measure the significance of any major artwork will suffer without some account of this context, this is uniquely the case when it comes to Guyton. However abstract his work may be on its surface, it is also strikingly and subtly in dialogue with its evolving cultural landscape. In fact, to gain a sense of the continuing arc of his work, one first has the job of going back, remembering and recovering the circumstances that made it possible. The current essay is therefore structured much like Guyton's canvases, folded over and divided into two parts, beginning with those dialogues of an earlier time before tracing the critical writings that would articulate his work's deep resonance within a larger cultural context.

* * *

No longer … not yet. I remember this evocative construction leaping out at me in 2009 when reading an obituary of the legendary Renaissance scholar Michael Baxandall, whose most influential volume, *Painting and Experience in Fifteenth-Century Italy: A Primer in the Social History of Pictorial Style* (1972), considered art-making at a cultural moment that seemed powerfully resonant with our own. Choosing provocatively in his study to take stock of painting in Quattrocento Italy merely as the "deposit of a social relationship," the scholar described a visual syntax as it developed among an urban populace whose everyday experience and perception was shaped and sustained by rapidly broadening channels of commerce and communication across increasingly vast geographies.[1] Artists of the time subsequently knew, Baxandall asserted, that they could rely on a particular kind of embodied eye among their audiences and patrons. All around them was a "common repertoire of skills, mental and affective habits, and bodily disciplines"—the ability to assess the volume of a barrel quickly, for example, or recognize configurations in courtly dance—with which the language of art would become uniquely interwoven in turn.[2] Yet most crucial for this remarkable relationship between art and experience— indeed, what made it possible at all—was its specific positioning within history. Or, perhaps more accurately, its uncertain position with respect to the very *idea* of history, coming about as it did during a flickering moment of possibility between the Middle Ages and modernity: in other words, after the clear reign of theological doctrine had dissipated, but before academicism and theory would appear during the next century and then persist in different forms through our time. As scholar Christopher Wood wrote of *Painting and Experience*, "In the 15th century, so it can seem in Baxandall's pages, artist and beholder met one another no longer under the supervision of the clergy, and not yet in the collector's cabinet or the museum."[3] Instead, they came together in the dynamic social space of the piazza, where so many methodologies were set in living and unsettled dialogue, with the predominant tenets of one receding culture put forward alongside those of another still arriving, and with artworks effectively providing figures of a present that—however much their meaning might be enriched when understood from one vantage or the other, or from both at once—belonged properly to neither.

At the particular juncture when I was reading these words, Baxandall's formulation would hardly have been called timely. The art world had grown exponentially during the previous decade, and to date seemed weirdly impervious to the effects of a global financial crisis. In fact, when it came to any question of uncertain temporalities and cultural impasses in artistic circles, of greater interest was the term *contemporary*—with practicing historians and critics in the field parsing, for instance, Giorgio Agamben's proposition that a work could belong to its moment yet remain at some distance from it. (The art world's sheer increase in size—especially among institutions, audiences, and markets devoted to emerging artists—was ostensibly propelling this investigation.) With the benefit of hindsight, however, one may reasonably consider whether the art world's infatuation with this nomenclature—and, in particular, with the philosopher's proposition that we might occupy a temporality that possesses an "out-of-jointness" by virtue of "a relationship with time that adheres to it through a disjunction and an anachronism"—suggested a liminal awareness of precisely the sort of paradigmatic shift described by Baxandall.[4] In other words, the very fascination with the "contemporary" bespoke a more nuanced loss of historical perspective—a sense of art's indeterminate place within any historical trajectory, and, in turn, an erosion of its habitual roles with respect to larger culture. While the art world's infrastructure (of museums and galleries, training-grounds and patrons) remained largely intact on its surface, the underlying models seemed tenuous nonetheless, as if at odds with another cultural logic that had not yet quite assumed form—imbuing a familiar landscape, conceived in the modern age, with a distantiated, representational quality. And against such a backdrop, Baxandall's proposition that we examine art's roots (and as important, its reception) in social realities would seem uniquely appropriate for surveying such a disoriented field.

In truth, many critics were wondering by the mid-1990s whether the very landscape and role of art had been subsumed by creative industries on a mass scale. Benefitting from the rise and expansion of media platforms online, as well as the enhanced flexibility and control of industrial production techniques, design culture had already assumed a decidedly more pronounced place in the popular conscience. Indeed, many of the pivotal developers within this commercial field had been trained by the very institutions producing the next generation of fine artists, meaning that numerous protagonists of this emerging industry were widely conversant in the very conceptual models once used to interrogate and resist forces of commodification. (The critical "miming" once attributed to artists engaging any "aesthetics of administration" could now take place within the commercial field itself.[5]) If a more circumscribed art world was relatively slow to articulate such shifting terms, by 2000 it was abundantly clear that even the most reflexive endeavors by postwar artists were at risk of merely becoming another decor in an expanding realm of commercial design. Asking around this time whether Minimalism had suffered such a fate, art historian Yve-Alain Bois would comment on its inevitability while wryly referring to a "Minimalist-art tour"—conducted by curators of the Guggenheim Museum no less—which promised stops at a restaurant designed by Richard Meier in Tribeca, and a Flavinesque window display at the then-new Apple Store in SoHo.[6] (The latter's structural morphing of gallery district into showrooms seemed a literal figure of art's emptied, shell-like attributes after being subsumed by mass enterprise.) Similarly, numerous theorists in architecture around the world at the turn of the millennium were observing how the forms and motifs of modernism were being widely employed in design, noting, however, that this reappearance was remarkably divorced from any symbolic program. The premises of an International Style at the beginnings of modernism during the 20th century had been evacuated, with no aspiration reflected beyond signifying and advancing the continuous circulation of information from point to point on the globe. As architectural theorist Hans Ibelings put it, such structures demonstrated "an architecture in which superficiality and neutrality have acquired special significance." The motifs of modernism were now deployed to convey not any message, but instead a kind of atmosphere, moving on from posing questions of place or context to denoting the idea of "boundless and undefined space" and the conduction of mobility.[7]

As if specifically in dialogue with such developments, multiple artists in both Europe and the United States began, around 2000, to incorporate modernist iconography in their work—regardless of medium, whether painting or sculpture, film or video—summoning those earlier programs even while underscoring their fundamental irretrievability. In this vein, art historian Hal Foster, writing in a seminal 2004 text that surveyed artistic production from the mid-1990s onward, titled "An Archival Impulse," would take partic-ular note of such artists seeking to "recoup failed visions in art" from the time of early modernism, saying that such efforts might "point to a general crisis in … social law—or to an important change in its workings whereby the symbolic order no longer operates through apparent totalities."[8] In other words, as artists such as Tacita Dean (Foster's example) stitched together fictional histories and utopias as stand-ins for those unrealized utopian aspirations during the previous century, they also underlined the absence of an overarching social and artistic program in the present day. Missing from the vocabulary of daily life—however much the fabric of social and economic organization was being rewoven globally after the historic political events of 1989—was an operative logic by which such aspirations might be implemented. (Such a tension was perhaps most readily apparent in presenta-tions and "re-presentations" of historical performance works —and even of political actions—associated with both early modernism and its descendants in postwar political and artistic engagement.[9]) Yet this loss of program extended to techniques typically associated with postmodernism as well.

Taking into account recent deployments of modernist forms and motifs primarily among European artists in a 2004 exhibition at the Kunstverein in Hamburg, *Formalismus. Moderne Kunst, heute*, critic and curator Diedrich Diederichsen observed that the very material shabbiness of their efforts on display underscored how such artists (including Sergej Jensen, Michael Krebber, and Katja Strunz, among others) intended to "[reexamine] the basic ideas of modernism in light of the very contemporary cognizance that every detail of presentation and production is likely already contaminated by specific histories."[10] Whereas modernist abstraction was once understood as a refuge from worldly concerns, it was by now imbricated in a "world choked with referentiality"— and its resurfacing here forced nothing less than a comprehensive reconsideration of how we "assign meaning to form" in the absence of any established guiding principles.[11]

In such a context, perhaps no artistic operation became so widespread—or contested—among a new generation as appropriation. Understood during the 1980s as a technique executed by artists who displaced images or objects from one context to another—thereby underlining that original setting's role in the construction of meaning, replete with hitherto implicit ideological biases—this function seemed by now to be continuously performed within a broader media infrastructure. Simply put, increasingly pervasive communication technologies and attending economies were developed specifically to support and enhance the perpetual circulation of information. Mirroring architecture's privileging of unfettered mobilization over place— and aided by digital tools facilitating familiarity with procedures of displacement throughout popular media, demonstrated even in the most domestic vocabularies of dragging and dropping, cutting and pasting onscreen— visual culture was increasingly characterized by a kind of depletion of information previously associated with appropriation. (The effects of this apparently free circulation quickly became a subject of widespread debate, with some public figures championing what they considered a newfound, liberative accessibility of cultural resources, and others protesting that such deterritorialized information would only give rise to cultural amnesia.) In turn, what had been a staple for artists coming of age during the postmodernist era—

with all its tenets of deconstruction and delineating of
"structures of signification," to borrow Douglas Crimp's
phase—risked becoming a style.[12] Indeed, in a sense,
just as models of circulation and exchange were becoming
drivers of economic value in larger culture, so they were
within the artistic sphere. The "sign" of criticality—the
mere action of moving an image or object from one context
to the next—was more valuable than any critical endeavor
in art that would actively problematize its surrounding
context. Put another way, the shift to decor that had taken
place within the sphere of Minimalist art now extended
to critical operations themselves—moving, in other words,
from object to activity. And while this dynamic was newly
apparent in sculpture and painting utilizing the motifs
of appropriation (as a device to signify critical engagement),
it had already been recognized by practitioners in other
mediums—as articulated by Andrea Fraser, for example,
when she considered the possibility that Institutional
Critique had itself been institutionalized by the mid-2000s,
reinscribing the very figures of authority its practitioners
had sought to question.[13] In fact, more than a decade before,
critic Isabelle Graw had suggested such a possibility when
surveying growing interest among museums in inviting
artists to interrogate their infrastructures and protocols,
calling such openness to interventions "subversion for hire."[14]

    This recasting of artistic endeavors typically associated
with antagonism toward cooptation and commodification
put into question the basic viability of critical models in art
—a kind of doubt that persists today. Celebrating the
journal *October*'s 100th issue in 2002, the publication's editors
wondered aloud whether "the radical idea that reproduction
can loosen the grip of the original … itself now falls victim
to reproduction's own exponential development within the
abyss of the cybernetic hall of mirrors."[15] Against this tide,
they proposed to take up Walter Benjamin's conception of
obsolescence, considering how outmoded mediums and
models might yet provide incisive perspectives on otherwise
all-enveloping and unquestioned technological progress—
and offer, in addition, a more resolved model with which to
grasp artists' recent embrace of modernist motifs in art as a
device for allowing critical distance. Yet this postulation was
but one of a number put forward by theorists and critics

surmising a cultural moment when skepticism regarding the efficacy of critical enterprises—at least as they were conventionally understood in the wake of modernism and its public sphere—corresponded with a pervasive sense that no historical trajectory in artistic discourse was clearly announcing itself. For a brief time, a few scholars proposed the notion of "after" as a term with which to describe the situation of art when its connection to modernist and postmodernist paradigms alike seemed strictly rhetorical.[16] By the conclusion of the millennium's first decade, however, these anxious disavowals of artistic teleology were eclipsed by curatorial engagements with encyclopedic and archaeological models, as many prominent exhibitions (and even art fairs) placed contemporary objects alongside ancient and prehistoric ones, and trained artists beside outsiders. The "archival impulse" displayed by artists some ten years prior—with all their fictional histories rehearsing the tropes of modernism in the hopes of reinvigorating a sense of potential in its program—had given way to a kind of de-historicizing of cultural production, with objects from different periods not suggesting any historical relation so much as seeming the stuff of sedimentary layering.[17] (The historical anachronism of our time had turned in character to idiosyncrasy.) And once this phenomenon had come to the fore, the art world would see—as did so many other disciplinary fields—a "material turn," which, in the words of Renaissance scholar Patricia Falguières, gave "new attention … to places and instruments, to apparatus, to the material nature of devices, and to objects."[18] The objects of art could not be seen apart "from the network of relations of which it is the guarantor, center, or vector"—at the same time, the subject (and subjectivity) could not be seen apart from the object—with one implication being that work was no longer strictly a matter of representation within the frame of art. As was the case during the brief moment described by Baxandall, it was now the matter of an altered, if also shared, experience.

＊＊＊

I rehearse this brief history of the 21st century in art because, time and again in writings on Wade Guyton (both in the present volume and elsewhere among journalistic and scholarly publications), authors will refer—as if in a kind of default setting—to incredible transitions taking place in culture. In fact, the various authors seeking to take account of Guyton's artistic practice in these pages are apt to speak just as much about his surrounding context. So it is that curator Daniel Baumann, for example, introducing the artist's early exhibition at the Kunstverein in Hamburg in 2005, asserts that modernism's conception of an "active viewer" is bound to "democratic bourgeois" social structures that are no longer sustainable—and it is Guyton's unique ability to create different blind spots in modern methodologies of interpretation, he says, that demonstrates how "[a]ll that no longer seems to work." Elsewhere, curator Scott Rothkopf, describing Guyton's use of appropriation in his first canvases—and wishing to distinguish the artist's approach from that of others employing modernist motifs in exhibitions such as the mentioned-above *Formalismus*— writes that Guyton understood his generation was "late not just to modernism's party but to postmodernism's, too. How then to figure this belatedness, to acknowledge a particular historicity while also charting a path forward?" (Guyton's answer, Rothkopf says, is to offer a kind of superimposition, subjecting the former party's iconography to the latter's strategies.[19] This sentiment is later echoed by Vincent Pécoil's observation that Guyton is inspired by "the tendency of art history books to transform abstraction into imagery.") More recently, art historian Bettina Funcke suggests that Guyton's move from paintings to large-scale room installations is of a piece with his peers' necessary desire to "redefine the place of art: its material and modes of production, reception, and dissemination." (In this respect, she says, audiences would do well to consider how we are witnessing the passage of one age to another, "moving from a physical to an increasingly digitized culture—and to an economy steeped in speculation.") Finally, and perhaps most granular in perspective, curator Achim Hochdörfer, reviewing Guyton's 2012 survey at the Whitney Museum of American Art, opens with the assertion that conventional constructions of modernity demand "decisive ruptures" that are, more accurately, "interregnums" in which "antithetical motives and genealogies can suddenly and surprisingly be connected with one another." In this sense, he says, Guyton's connection with his cultural moment may be compared to that of Jasper Johns, whose work similarly "looks back to one period as it looks forward to another." While for Johns such an "easy congruence" invited associations with Dada, Minimalism, and Abstract Expressionism all at once, for Guyton—whose emergence saw "the first signs of the disintegration of the critical formation of the 1990s"—this allowed for the intermingling, in the minds of audiences encountering his work, of high modernism and commercial design, preindustrial and postindustrial methods, Minimalism and Pop, appropriation and institutional critique.

Indeed, readers here might gain a strikingly textured sense of Guyton's intellectual times through these writings. The pieces in this volume often reflect on their discursive context with incredible nuance, even registering minute changes in conversations taking place within the art world from year to year. (The specificity can be remarkable, with readings of Guyton's work set in nearly seismographic dialogue with the art world's shifting interests in, say, post-Fordism; or the effects of a vastly expanded art market; or, in a more scholarly vein of intellectual history, the first translation of Roland Barthes' *The Neutral* into English in 2005.) Partly this variegation has to do with the particular collection of voices found in this volume: one would be hard-pressed to find such a spectrum of perspectives among people who, whatever their contrasting approaches to art—from the connoisseurial and formalist to speculative and materialist—were in such active and engaged dialogue with each other, whatever cities they might have been calling home across the globe. It is one of Guyton's unique attributes as an artist that he has been able to mobilize so many authors around his practice and, perhaps, a fleeting bit of art history that all these lives were so entwined during the relatively brief period covered in these pages. And, in fact, this ability has hardly gone unnoticed. In his review of Guyton's Whitney survey, for example, Hochdörfer felt it necessary to mention that the artist "is embedded in a broad network of artist friends, critics, curators, gallerists, and collectors"—which might lend some credence to David Joselit's 2009 argument in his essay "Painting Beside Itself," not published in this volume, that painting is a "transitive" object whose crucial interface is with the social setting in which it is situated.[20] Of course, here one might also recall Baxandall's piazza, even if conversation among contributors here was happening online and in magazines, as well as through the occasional stint as an invited lecturer abroad.

Yet these correspondences between Guyton's production and its surrounding context are much more telling with respect to his seeming apprehension about any fixed meaning that might be ascribed to his work. In this vein, art historian and critic Johanna Burton—writing in one of the earliest texts devoted to Guyton, titled "Such Uneventful Events" (2004)—astutely recalls Roland Barthes' assertion that the markings of Cy Twombly's calligraphic compositions are "decipherable but not interpretable." As Barthes says of those earlier works, which readily summon readings but are never reconciled with them: "What is performed is culture itself—or, rather, the gestures and ciphers of culture. [The paintings' markings] are not messages themselves but instead the gestures of message."[21] In other words, Twombly's canvases frustrate the very readings they invite, prompting viewers to reconsider the meanings they bring to the work merely by being members of a given culture structuring experience; the frequently de facto procedures by which significance is assigned become as much the object of contemplation as any aesthetic material placed before the eye. Such reflections are similarly to be found in Guyton's compositions. As Burton writes, "meaning sticks to them"; and any viewer of their various appropriations of modernist form "risks slipping into representational roll-call (and role-playing)" that "[i]ronically calls attention to historical knowledge—and our reliance on it in performing comfortable acts of calcifying interpretation." Intriguingly, this call-and-effect might be all the more evident at a historical juncture when, as Burton says more pointedly, historical conventions of meaning-making have stopped functioning, and "avant-garde and capitalist strategies spanning Naum Gabo to Minimalism to suede couch module have all evolved into kitsch goods equally well." The stylization of critical procedures in art underscores—and extends—the very circulation of their motifs.

Guyton's work is subsequently populated throughout by slippages—or better, by sliding signifiers. If I observe, in my own republished text from 2003, that "Guyton marks the spot of his art historical origins and defaces it at the same time," the letter "X" to which I refer turns, by the time of Burton's writing, to the more ambiguous (and humorous) letter "U." Not long thereafter, the place in his works occupied by such signs is given over to red and green stripes, which Rothkopf argues, resolve themselves neither as representation nor as abstraction, to say nothing of pure materiality. (Couching his remarks in terms of Guyton's decision-making in the studio, Rothkopf says: "He needed a sign that could operate at once as an image and as an abstract element that could be coopted and redeployed without getting bogged down in specific reference or subject matter.") Along similar lines, other authors like Pécoil will note how Guyton's *Untitled Action Sculptures* are both gestural and abstract, and retain their identity as disfigured elements of Breuer chairs even while they are put forward as sculptural abstraction. (Such matters open onto the obsessiveness with which some observers would ask whether or not Guyton's canvases are truly "paintings.") It is only fitting by the end of this collection that a couple authors—Burton and John Kelsey—eventually deploy Barthes' *The Neutral*, in which the theorist indicates that his title's chosen term pertains to "every inflection that, dodging or baffling the paradigmatic, oppositional structure of meaning, aims at the suspension of the conflictual basis of discourse."[22] Gone, in other words, are binaries, negations, and nullifications of modernism. Instead, figures of the neutral never settle into a singular, readable position. As Burton suggests in her later text, "Rites of Silence," Guyton seems throughout his practice to proceed by way of so many impasses, but only while "[s]eeming foreclosures are levied to hold open future possibilities."[23]

Such an orientation toward future possibilities would certainly open Guyton to criticisms, and seemingly even among his champions, with regard to his relationship with questions of circulation and, more specifically, packaging to ensure his work's continual movement. (Appropriation in the past consisted of a displacement to unveil the unspoken assumptions and biases of a given place; but now such displacements seemed turned toward future possibilities.) While reflecting the vantage of a particular socioeconomic moment in which the distinctions of work and life were being newly blurred, Kelsey's "Decapitalism," penned on the occasion of a pivotal exhibition of Guyton with Seth Price, Josh Smith, and Kelley Walker at Kunsthalle Zürich, proposes that "their grouping is at least partly a European construction. It is their packaging and touring as Guyton, Price, Walker, Smith that allows for the production of something like a New York moment in the Kunsthalle, or wherever such moments are in demand." A few years later, in "100%," Kelsey observes how Guyton will present the same body of work—and even promotional posters for exhibitions—in different gallery booths of the same art fair, effectively incorporating advertisements for his practice within more conventional work. Whereas Rothkopf sees Guyton's engagement with exhibition posters, labels, and book jackets in terms of a postmodern legacy—Guyton is here a child of Louise Lawler, in a sense—Kelsey argues that such attention to framing has by now extended to the artist him- or herself, rendering such historical terms for critique unstable: "Like any worker today, the artist's job is also to talk and to move, putting words, images, and his own body into circulation." (Notably in this "connexionist" vein, Kelsey provocatively describes Guyton's studio as a "quasi-office" given its dependency on desktop computers, which both produce the work on nearby printers and connect the artist with his distribution network among galleries and collectors.) While, for some, Guyton's black monochromes are effective precisely for "not quite getting there," as Burton puts it, for Kelsey the "monochrome is a record of circulation … [and] 100% black is the most a machine of an artist can say, do, or send, a total saturation and total activation of the space of communication."

Conversations around abstraction and circulation like these are, in fact, strongly reminiscent of postmodern discourse during the 1980s. For example, writing in the catalogue accompanying the 1986 exhibition *Endgame* at the Institute of Contemporary Art, Boston, art historian Thomas Crow noted how the concept of art was being sustained in the face of commercial forces precisely by virtue of being "weak"—with artists ceding their authorial agency and subjecting their work, and particularly their efforts in abstraction, to "endless rearrangement and repackaging."[24] Most pertinent for Guyton in this light, however, is Crow's observation regarding artists' disposition when recognizing that "if abstract art once had served as a haven of authentic experience in a visual world dominated by meretricious distractions and seductions, it can no longer serve that function."[25] For artists like Sherrie Levine, he says, their work suggests "the uneasy death of modernism" as she "gesture[s] back … to a time when painting seems to have been able confidently to articulate a culture's shared beliefs."[26] Such an assessment resonates strongly with a conversation between Burton and *Texte zur Kunst* editor Isabelle Graw. Responding to the latter's argument that "appropriation today has developed into a kind of referentialism," Burton responds: "[Guyton] actually poses the question about this kind of comfort we have today with constantly circulating signs. Less than feeling comfortable … his work often professes a real anxiety, and doesn't feel that it actually belongs in the history it invokes at all."[27] This unease also finds a partner in Rothkopf's professed sense of belatedness imbuing the artist's various objects.

It then might well be that the deconstruction of the author by a previous generation of artists gives way, in Guyton's work, to a kind of abnegation of the author. Put another way, it gives way to a recognition of the author's necessary imbrication not merely within any representational paradigm (the cemetery containing the "death of the author," as it were), but also within a material environment. Indeed, if the theorist Flusser—cited here by Kelsey—argues that the "photographer is first of all already a function of the camera's program" (making distinctions of subject and object more indistinct), so it is that Guyton frequently allows material circumstances, of both culture and technology, to guide his production. Such conditions might themselves even be said to constitute the apparatus of production, not only making gestures decipherable within their confines—in accordance with remarks decades ago by Hans Haacke, who described the reliance of any critical gesture on its institutional framework for legibility— but also shaping the very material reality of those gestures. In fact the true extent of such authorial deference is continually a subject of subtle debate around Guyton. Numerous writers underline how his formal decisions are often steered by technological parameters, whether with respect to printer widths or the viscosity of inks, for instance. In the most recent essay here—Funcke's essay titled "Reclaimed Zones: Guyton's Rooms"—the writer observes how the scale of artist's massive canvases are determined by the architecture within which they find themselves. She quotes the artist regarding his larger works in 2014 gallery exhibitions at Friedrich Petzel and Chantal Crousel: "I did think I was letting the black paintings 'un-become' paintings, or express themselves more architecturally. Or let the building or the spaces determine where the paintings should end and relate to each other. And allow those pressures to give form to the work." Such a remark is tied easily enough to Guyton's repeated emphasis on the role of accident in his work. (What comes to mind is Jean Genet's comparison of writing, in *Prisoner of Love*, to the practice of Japanese vase-makers who develop their vessels around structural flaws encountered at the very beginning of their endeavors.) But references to Guyton's process and, moreover, the staging of Guyton's tussles and forced errors with his printers in the studio—where the digital medium physically meets the analogue artist—risk reinscribing the terms of artistic mastery by default. Among the few articles republished here from the popular press, Peter Schjeldahl's profile of the artist is noteworthy for being the first and only to include biographical detail alongside discussions of the artist's deep interest in printer errors—as when Guyton says his procedures are getting more difficult, because printers are "getting better" in their auto-corrections. The implicit debate around Guyton's mastery, in other words, revolves to an extent around whether the altered terms of the artist's studio suggest a paradigmatic shift in art and culture, after all. Or is this "new" studio fundamentally the same, and merely populated by technologies that are only another set of tools?

Perhaps such a discussion opens onto much larger questions about the state of things in contemporary society, prompting broader reflections on the relationship between any creative individual and the surrounding environment and, more precisely, marking a shift in the basis for our distinguishing between them in any conventional mode. In fact, the possibility that Guyton's practice signals a change in the fundamental understanding of materiality is articulated most clearly here as Funcke's discussion of Guyton's "rooms" appears alongside a text by Catherine Chevalier. The latter casts Guyton's installations not in terms of representation but instead of material (rendered through pressure, like grooves in a record), before considering the artist's decision in 2014 to install a new series of paintings at Galerie Chantal Crousel in Paris that was arranged to look precisely like his exhibition there just six years before, ensuring that audiences experience the second iteration in a novel way. Likely to have first seen the exhibition in images elsewhere, audiences encounter the physical space, as well as the works contained therein, as if in a kind of déjà vu. And to explain, Chevalier paraphrases philosopher Paolo Virno's assertion that we are—as images are increasingly divorced from their referents throughout culture—witnessing the rise of "a new contemporary mneumonic pathology whose symptoms are to be found in the quasi-concomitance of experience and its representation on social networks such as Instagram, Facebook, and Twitter ... The risk would be for the viewer to be distanced from immediate, personal perception, with the disconcerting feeling of having experienced it before. But in another manner." In short, a kind of false memory rises to the fore. And the historical implications of this dynamic for art become clearer as Guyton locates the Crousel iteration of his project in technological terms: "This time, the photos we took of the exhibition, the memory of the exhibition, and the exhibition itself become templates that can be reprinted, reactivated, reperformed ... So a return to that exhibition as a file." The artist's summation suggests a kind of displacement through circulation that recalls the precedent of appropriation during the 1980s. However, those earlier efforts continually revolved around displacing some preexisting image or object—something from the past, and whose history could be teased out— whereas Guyton's model of a "file" is oriented toward the future. His work anticipates its own circulation and displacement, and even courts such displacement in advance of the audience's experience.

In this respect, what seems a paradigmatic shift in culture—and one with tumultuous consequences, given the increasing distance set between reality and representation—

might register even within single works. To speak first in formal terms, Guyton is hardly alone among artists of his generation introducing new applications to historical procedures such as appropriation, even affecting changes in temporality and, in turn, the psychological character of their artwork. To offer a key example illustrating the latter: in the essay accompanying Douglas Crimp's famous 1977 *Pictures* exhibition, the critic takes up the example of Jack Goldstein's *Fencers* to discuss the "paradoxical mechanism by which memory functions … image is gradually forgotten, altered, replaced."[28] The image, he says, then becomes psychological—the stuff of memory and personal history—in the wake of its disappearance. More recently, however, artists have moved away from engaging such a sequence of events as it pertains to the displacements of appropriation. Instead of teasing out the information embedded in an image, object, or physical site—presenting in their work what happens "after" the displacement—artists frequently present kinds of displacements that might yet occur, focusing on the moments "before" meaning has resolved.[29] (The attendant sense of déjà vu finds a phenomenological corollary in Kelsey's description of audiences' bodies walking through Guyton's gallery spaces modeled after his studio: the black space looks stable, yet the material texture is anything but.) Indeed, looking at contemporary media infrastructures, one finds that the operation by which something has been "forgotten" and "replaced" has occurred in advance of our arrival on the scene.

In many of this works, Guyton's anticipation of images' circulation—as well as his incorporation of circulation into the most fundamental, material fabric of the work—reflects such a reversal of terms. Yet the stakes for this reorientation of time is perhaps made plainest in his most recent canvases featuring screen shots of the *New York Times*. Populated by news items that are ostensibly steeped in exterior events from the past, they nevertheless reflect a reorientation of time throughout contemporary culture as it has been shaped by technology—forcing a consideration, for instance, of how algorithms track one's browsing habits online, such that whatever one chooses to see draws similar and related information to one's screen. The question of "authorship" here becomes very ambiguous, with different news items—and advertisements—having gravitated to Guyton's browser. (Images are less measures of expression than of action; or better, one's actions summon expressivity that provided from without.) Through such real-time customization, one's very history, in fact, may seem to come from without, arriving in advance of experience.[30] Significantly enough, the artist's name appears on the printed canvas not in any conventional authorial signature, but as a "sign-in"—an opened portal to circulatory networks of information.

These canvases are subsequently all the more interesting for making literal, and even narrative, what had been liminal in his work to date: a material reflection of the culture of which it is a part. Examining one of his recent canvases from December 1, 2015 (reproduced on page 4), is like reading so many social hieroglyphs. With a seam running vertically down the canvas' middle, the work features a kind of uneven screen roll on its face, seeming a literal figure of our contemporary "out-of-jointness." (The dividing line—variously called a zip or navel by writers on his work—provides Guyton's usual material evidence of the painting's creation by running a folded canvas through the printer, with each side receiving ink consecutively. But the disruptive impact on information is clearer now that the canvas surface contains figuration.) The different, sometimes fragmented headlines are discrete in their subjects, yet their juxtapositions nevertheless invite a projection of interrelation, whether regarding a report on police brutality in Chicago or another describing the Grand Old Party's paralysis in the face of Donald Trump's resilience within the party's primaries; an article on a right-wing extremist's attack on Planned Parenthood or unfolding climate talks in Paris. A cultural syntax begins to emerge. And, crucially, the perfect term to describe this patterning of information appears in an advertisement dominating both the *New York Times'* homepage and the composition of Guyton's painting: *nexus*, a term pertaining to connections, or networks, of causal links among different points or groups, which has been harnessed here as the brand name of a new smartphone whose technological cipher is, after all, designed to coordinate and navigate such complex relationships. Guyton's previous abstractions in art might have been deeply correlated with social developments—with cultural meaning drawn to them across the years—but here they give way to the abstractions of culture itself, with abstraction and realism finally becoming one and the same. And, as pointedly when it comes to uncertain histories, reports of things past are also harbingers of things to come.

[1] See Christopher S. Wood, "When Attitudes Became Form," *Artforum* (January 2009), p. 43.

[2] Ibid., p. 44.

[3] Ibid.

[4] Giorgio Agamben, "What is the Contemporary?" *What is an Apparatus? and Other Essays*, Stanford University Press, Stanford 2009, p. 39–54, here p. 40–41.

[5] See Benjamin H. D. Buchloh, "Conceptual Art 1962–1969: From the Aesthetic of Administration to the Critique of Institutions," *October* 55 (Winter 1990), p. 105–143.

[6] See Yve-Alain Bois, "Specific Objections: Three Exhibitions," *Artforum* (Summer 2004).

[7] See Hans Ibelings, *Supermodernism: Architecture in the Age of Globalization*, Netherlands Architecture Institute, Rotterdam 1998. The volume is a somewhat slight but useful overview of architectural thinking at the time, indebted as well to Marc Augé's concept of the "non-place"—a transient space of relative anonymity, from airports to hotel lobbies—upon which he expands. To my mind, however, one of the most remarkable statements about abstraction was made by Robert Pincus Witten in relation to the rise of painterly abstraction during the 20th century: "By the mid-20th century, abstraction had all but defeated representational art, and all the learned arcana of past centuries ended up as the familiar Untitled Abstraction, work about which we need know nothing in order to accept or reject it. The Untitled Abstraction is arguably one of the great achievements of capitalist democracy. While you did not have to know anything, you still had to allow yourself to be acted upon, and allow yourself to be open to the purely visual or formal stimuli of the work. This development paralleled the rise of psychotherapeutic methods—so that we *really* could be open—as well as a great perplexity about modern art: people thought abstraction was difficult precisely because it 'had no subject matter.'" And precisely such absence of subject matter allowed the mode to circulate more freely as a commodity. See "Art and Its Markets: A Roundtable Discussion," *Artforum* (April 2008), p. 292–303.

[8] Hal Foster, "An Archival Impulse," *October* 110 (Autumn 2004), p. 21–22.

[9] Guyton himself would occasionally present reenactments of historical dialogues from art during the mid-2000s (Bettina Funcke briefly discusses such work in her text in this volume). But an incisive discussion of the phenomenon more broadly may be found in some of scholar Hal Foster's criticism of artist Jeremy Deller, for which the scholar offers the proposition *pre-posterous*, meaning to underscore temporalities held in suspension, never resolving into relationships of "pre-" or "post-." See Hal Foster, "History is a Hen Harrier," *Jeremy Deller: English Magic*, exh. cat., British Council, London 2013, p. 15.

[10] Diedrich Diederichsen, "Formalismus," *Artforum* (March 2005), p. 231.

[11] Ibid.

[12] See Douglas Crimp, *Pictures*, exh. cat., Artists Space, New York 1977.

[13] See Andrea Fraser, "From the Critique of Institutions to an Institution of Critique," *Artforum* (September 2005), p. 278–283, 332.

[14] See Isabelle Graw, "Field Work," *Flash Art* (November–December 1990), p. 137.

[15] Rosalind Krauss and George Baker, "Introduction," *October*, 100 (Spring 2002), p. 3–5, here p. 3.

[16] While numerous scholars employed such wording at the time, two relevant examples in publishing include Pamela M. Lee's *Forgetting the Art World*, MIT Press, Cambridge, Massachusetts 2012—she would also pen an essay, "After Obsolescence"—and David Joselit's *After Art*, Princeton University Press, Princeton, New Jersey 2012.

[17] See Tim Griffin, "From Art to Artifact," *Parkett* 95 (2014), p. 164–170.

[18] Patricia Falguières, "Fatal Attraction," in Tim Griffin (ed.), *The New Existentialism*, Les presses du réel, Dijon 2017, n.p.

[19] Looking for historical footing after postmodernism's overturning of modernism, Rothkopf makes a more poignant and even urgent assertion: "One beauty—and potential pathos—of Guyton's method is his very questioning of how one might convincingly impose limits on a practice at a time when there would otherwise seem to be none."

[20] See David Joselit, "Painting Beside Itself," *October* 130 (Fall 2009), p. 125–134.

[21] See Roland Barthes, "Non Multa Sed Multum," Nicola del Roscio (ed.), *Writings on Cy Twombly*, Schirmer/Mosel, Munich 2002, p. 88–113.

[22] See Roland Barthes, *The Neutral*, ed. Thomas Clerc, trans. Rosalind E. Krauss and Denis Hollier, Columbia University Press, New York 2005, p. 211.

[23] In contradistinction to such impasses, the author also notably underlines how Guyton's work strongly flirts with the subtle social question of just what it means to "pass."

[24] Thomas Crow, "The Return of Hank Heron," *Endgame: Reference and Simulation in Recent Painting and Sculpture*, exh. cat., Institute of Contemporary Art, Boston 1986, p. 16.

[25] Ibid., p. 15.

[26] Ibid. If Levine demonstrates an anxious acceptance of modernism's dwindling returns, that disposition prompted her to recast originals, acknowledging her distance from modernism, and putting her desire for their viability, and veracity, on display. Something similar may be said of Guyton.

[27] Johanna Burton and Isabelle Graw, "When Procedures Become Market Tools: A Conversation with Johanna Burton by Isabelle Graw," *Texte zur Kunst* 62 (June 2006), p. 186.

[28] Douglas Crimp, *Pictures*, exh. cat., Artists Space, New York 1977, p. 6.

[29] In my 2011 essay "Compression," I offer the illustration of artist Pierre Huyghe speaking of his 1995 work *Casting*, which consisted of a casting call to which both actors and audiences were invited: "It was impossible to know who were the visitors to the exhibition and who were the actors for the film. *It is the moment before an image.*" See Tim Griffin, "Compression," *October* 135 (Winter 2011), p. 3–20.

[30] I write on this phenomenon more at length in "Notes on an Art Domain," *Texte zur Kunst* (September 2012), p. 140–155.

First Take On Wade Guyton
Tim Griffin

Originally published in *Artforum*, vol. 41, no. 5, January 2003, p. 126.

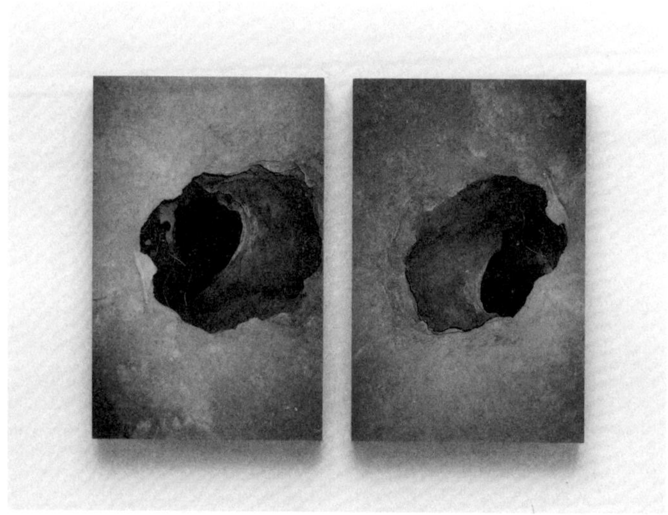

The Devil's Hole (left and right), 1999
Two chromogenic prints mounted on wood, 75.2 × 49.5 × 4.6 cm each

Wade Guyton has referred to his sculptures as drawings in space. No doubt this assertion has something to do with his three-dimensional works' frequent status as studies. (Indeed, in the past couple of years Guyton has made a number of pieces individually titled *Fragment of Sculpture the Size of a House*, each corresponding to a structural component of the suburban home the artist intends to construct and paint completely black, sometime in the future.) Yet his statement has as much to do with the physical character of the objects, which can seem crudely superimposed on space, at once underscoring the sculptural aspect of *seeing* and demonstrating Guyton's interest in the dynamics of sculpture transposed across media. In his *Fragments* (2000), for example, the artist inserts into the gallery environment a large aluminum-and-plywood plane whose irregular geometry and matte black surface interrupt the sight lines and flow of light through the room. The object's severe angles are totally incongruous with the surroundings, composing a form that apparently slices through space or, more accurately, blots it out like ink on paper. It is a brilliant kind of dead-zone sculpture: if Gordon Matta-Clark generated disruptions of space by eliminating portions of the built environment—incising the walls or floors, even chainsawing an entire house in half—Guyton does the same using an additive process.

Inspired in part by the odd flattening of his sculptures when they are reproduced in pictures, the artist has lately made a number of "printer drawings," which will appear in March [2003] at Artists Space in New York. These consist of simple patterns printed on photographs taken from art and interior design books of the 1970s and 1980s. A massive "X" hovers above viewers contemplating a Minimalist sculpture in a gallery at the Walker Art Center in one drawing. In another, a sequence of "X"s runs across the image of a public sculpture by Charles Ginnever [sculptor, b. 1931]. (Guyton marks the spot of his art historical origins and defaces it at the same time.) Elsewhere, one sees how the page might be considered simply one more viewing plane in space: some drawings depict "X"s to be placed in windows, blocking the perspectival view, crossing out the landscape as if it were merely a picture. Paper becomes glass, while art history, represented in Guyton's copies, turns into decor.

Decor is nothing if not desire sublimated into the living environment, and Guyton's works, which are often strangely anthropomorphic, harbor deep psychological charges. The inanimate borders on the animate, whether objects or art history. The dead is somehow alive in Guyton's hands. Perhaps that tension arises from the artist's youth. Raised on slasher flicks—as a child in the 1970s, every Friday he went with his parents to the drive-ins around Knoxville, Tennessee—he admits that his project for a suburban home may have been partially inspired by the bucket-of-blood thriller *The Last House on the Left* (1972). The shining blades of other such celluloid dwellings also come to mind when one considers Guyton's columns made of vertical strips of black Plexiglas and mirrored acrylic in gold, smoke, and bronze. The angular works seem to have knifed up violently through the ground. And, as viewers move, reflective surfaces make the sculptures seem to expand and contract as if alive,

both consuming architectural space and disappearing into it
(with murderous logic).

If there is a telltale heart buried within this practice,
one photographic diptych from 1999 might be it: the pair
depicts the Devil's Hole, a small cavern in Tennessee. The
deep focus on rippling rock surfaces makes the pictures
verge on abstraction, and lurid inflections of red light and
sub-zero flecks of turquoise create a pictorial paradox, with
the tunnel at once cold and hot. Stark walls seem sensuous,
providing an analogy for all of Guyton's work, which resusci-
tates a Minimalism whose heart is still beating under art
history's floorboards. Guyton may have made photographs
in caves, but there is no way he will remain underground
for long.

Such Uneventful Events:
The Work of Wade Guyton
Johanna Burton

Originally published in Yilmaz Dziewior (ed.), *Formalism. Modern Art, Today*, exh. cat., Kunstverein in Hamburg, Hamburg, October 9, 2004–January 9, 2005, Hatje Cantz, Ostfildern 2004, p. 54–61.

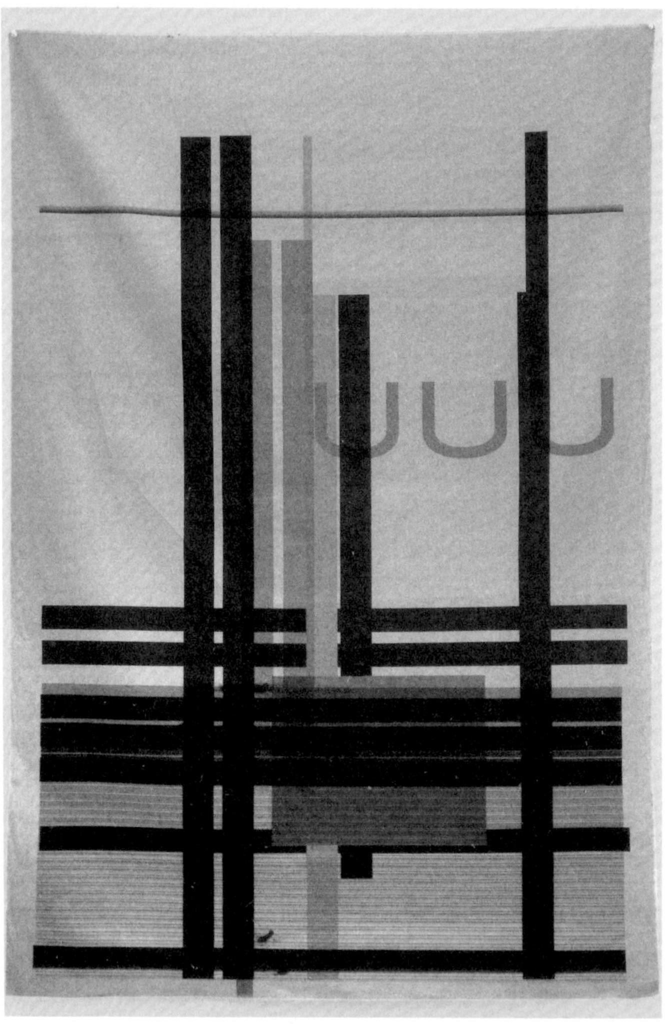

Untitled, 2005
Epson UltraChrome inkjet on linen, 162.9 × 104.5 cm

"Meaning sticks to man: even when he wants to create non-meaning or extra-meaning, he ends by producing the very meaning of non-meaning or of extra-meaning."
—Roland Barthes

I.

Roland Barthes begins his 1979 *The Wisdom of Art* (an essay that ultimately equates Cy Twombly's procedures with Zen philosophies) with the following speculation: "Whatever the transformations of painting, whatever its substance and its context, the same question is always asked: *What is happening here?*" Some 25 years after Harold Rosenberg had dubbed the Ab-Ex canvas "an arena in which to act," and nearly a decade after Michael Fried posited what he saw as the insidious outcome of such a notion within the "literal" bodies of minimalist sculpture, Barthes takes Twombly as a muse "decipherable but not interpretable," likening

his work to an altogether different theatrical "event," for
which the basis is neither Aristotelian nor phenomenological
but, rather, textual.

In the Twomblinian drama, what is performed is
culture itself—or, rather, the gestures and ciphers of culture,
themselves blatantly uninterested in passing for more (or
less) than citation. Scrawled pictograms—hybrid text-images
—call up classical references from Leonardo da Vinci to
Nicolas Poussin to Paul Valéry, but only to represent the
structural functions of allusion, representation, and content.
And these let viewers/readers "content" themselves, albeit
momentarily, with falling into (and onto) their own vast
personal archives of knowledge (these plucked from the
"abîme" of culture). But then really *look* at, say, Twombly's
Age of Alexander (1959–1960), Barthes implores us, and considers its titular and pictorial references (which he reminds
us, are not messages themselves but instead the gestures
of message). The allusion (but never acquiescence) toward
meaning bears its load like a chimera—at once delivering
too much and not nearly enough. Such a conscious parting
of the curtains reinstalls what Barthes terms "vagueness":
(that feeling so familiar to poets) where one knows one knows
but one does not know *what*. This is an Event.

II.

Now, what is happening here? Wade Guyton's most recent
works—still in process, perpetually in process—hang in
the studio, unstretched, layered out of spatial necessity
(which forces a spontaneous formal dialogue between them
that feels, nonetheless, warranted). These are, ostensibly,
paintings, though there is no recourse to paint as such
("painted" as they are by ink-jet printer) and the support,
while admittedly canvas, announces itself equally well as
tapestry, fabric, tablecloth: the limp material denigrates any
usual high-art pretense and instead reveals itself as embarrassingly unaccounted for, failing to convert either to representational illusion or "pure" materiality. The execution is
similarly unsettled; there is no sign of authorial mark—even
by way of the deeply authorial non-authorship of the drip,
stain, pour, puddle, or field. Still, there are painterly asides
to be identified here, in these "gauche" approximations of

paintings (Barthes reminds us that our word for lack of social grace is etymologically traced to the awkward aesthetics associated with lefthanded mark making. Perhaps, as Warhol illustrates, *no*-handed production is the most gauche of all). There are flat, lusterless, yet unexpectedly pleasing colors and shapes that are immediately recognizable, if not interpretable. They are too easily generalized to be attributed to any singular context and, because of this, are not naturally of any context at all: circles, squares, thick stripes alone or crisscrossed in grids and isolated or clustered horseshoes that are clearly themselves culled from the well of language— the letter "U" in no-frills Blair ITC Medium font, snatched from semiotic utility and blown up to various scales by plugging in ridiculously large font-size numbers (anywhere from 500 to 1500). By perverse logic, these are personal statements devoid of personality.

Guyton's "printer paintings" might be described, paradoxically enough, as surprisingly boring. They are made by plotting out abstract, if not entirely non-representational compositions on the computer screen and then feeding lengths of 44-inch wide (maximum) canvas through an industrial printer. The resulting paintings seem, at first, to demurely cite the effects and condition of their own self-conscious production, with little reference to anything else. Indeed, the limitations of the printer determine certain structural principles, these writ large on the paintings. No work can exceed the dimension of the machine's width, but theoretically can be as long as an entire bolt of linen. (One can imagine Guyton sending rerolled bolts of the stuff to be cut and hung like wallpaper in site-specific exhibitions, as Warhol did with his lengths of silk-screened silver-and-black Elvises.) In addition, while there is no limit to the color mixing capabilities of the enormous ink-jet, Guyton often chooses to pair his primary objects with primary colors.

One would assume the "printer paintings," then, to be so many mechanically reproduced—and reproducible— contemporary formal arrangements, reviving Stella's will to "what you see is what you see." Yet, Guyton's "printer paintings" instead invoke the necessary dialectic between what one sees and what one does not as well as what operates smoothly and what goes serendipitously wrong. (The best of the bunch bear the scars of literal malfunctions—snagged or muddled canvas, under- or over-saturated inks, blurred or bumped outlines.) If these are Events in the Barthesian sense (which I think they are), they are "slow" events, nearly uneventful, but nonetheless dramatic. Similarly auspicious derailings have persistently defined Guyton's work, who has in the past built stages too large to comfortably hold objects, too small to comfortably hold people, just awkward enough to impede easy movement through a room; and shoddy folding structures made of tacky bronze, silver, gold, and black Plexiglas—works that allude to an interior but quickly reveal themselves to be dumb examples of (literally) sheer surface, Minimalism rendered as a deep pleat. The artist has de- and reconstructed that totem of Modernist design, the Breuer chair, so that its limbs flail toward the respectable utility it continues to signify even while disabled from proffering; and his own version of a Dan Graham pavilion, reduced to a surfaceless skeleton structure that passively refuses the reflectivity (and reflexivity) of the original.

In addition, Guyton has continued to produce literal realms of an ongoing series referred to as "printer drawings," these the more outspoken cousins to the "printer paintings" that follow them. Ripping pages from design, architecture, and art magazines from the 1920s to the 1980s and running them through his printer (this the unexceptional cheap model found in nearly every home-office), Guyton marries trails of ambiguous signification culled from Word and Photoshop to glossy pages representing just-past aesthetic histories. Geometric forms and letters rendered dully decorative through repetition are printed on top of images of sculptures, large-scale public art, interior design, and buildings (timber frame to Farnsworth House). For a time, the artist's cipher of choice was an enormous "X" (also in Blair font), but when it became clear that the illiteracy of intention he strove for was too easily trumped (X = a simultaneous marking of and marking out was the overwhelmingly agreed upon critical interpretation), Guyton opted for another letter, "U"— this both much more difficult and yet seemingly simpler to assign meaning to (a sliding signifier applicable to everyone, and thus, to no one in particular). The "printer drawings" are an enduring experiment, in which palimpsests of image and indeterminate semiotic signs are tested for the literal elasticity of signification they produce. The "printer paintings," then, perform as a limit case in this experiment, withdrawing altogether the "referential" images assumed to be ambivalent site of homage and defacement in the drawings.

Guyton's "printer paintings" decidedly *don't do* very much (in fact, they risk embarrassment to do so little) and yet it is precisely this delicious vagueness that lays bare the impulse—and the shortcomings—of same-same meaning making. Doing away with the coded imagery that literally provided a base for the drawings, Guyton effectively leaves us with paintings that are propositions, onesided suspended dialogues between an artist and a withheld (though we can still accurately guess the contents) cultural archive. What is visible in the "printer paintings," then, is a bare bones Morse code born of an acknowledgment that avant-garde and capitalist strategies spanning Naum Gabo to Minimalism to suede couch modules, have all evolved into kitsch fetish goods equally well. Appropriated images, Guyton wagers, sometimes risks slipping into representational roll-call (and role-playing); alluding to the "abîme" of culture without calling forward its representatives is perhaps one way to disallow the contentment of content. By decidedly not including such references in these recent works (while addressing them nonetheless), Guyton ironically calls atten-tion to historical knowledges—and our reliance on them in performing comfortable acts of calcifying interpretation. (Even still, I had to quickly check the first [defensive] reaction I had to the "printer paintings": a quick rifle through my version of the art history archive—surely these works bore useful similarities to Constructivism, to Bauhaus … Then I reminded myself. It is hardly worth asking, "What is happening here?" if you are convinced that you already know.)

New Forms of Modernism;
Ambivalence and Ambiguity;
'An Act of Processing'
Kirsty Bell

Originally published as "Focus: Wade Guyton. New Forms of Modernism; Ambivalence and Ambiguity; 'An Act of Processing,'" in *Frieze*, no. 93, September 2005, p. 55–61

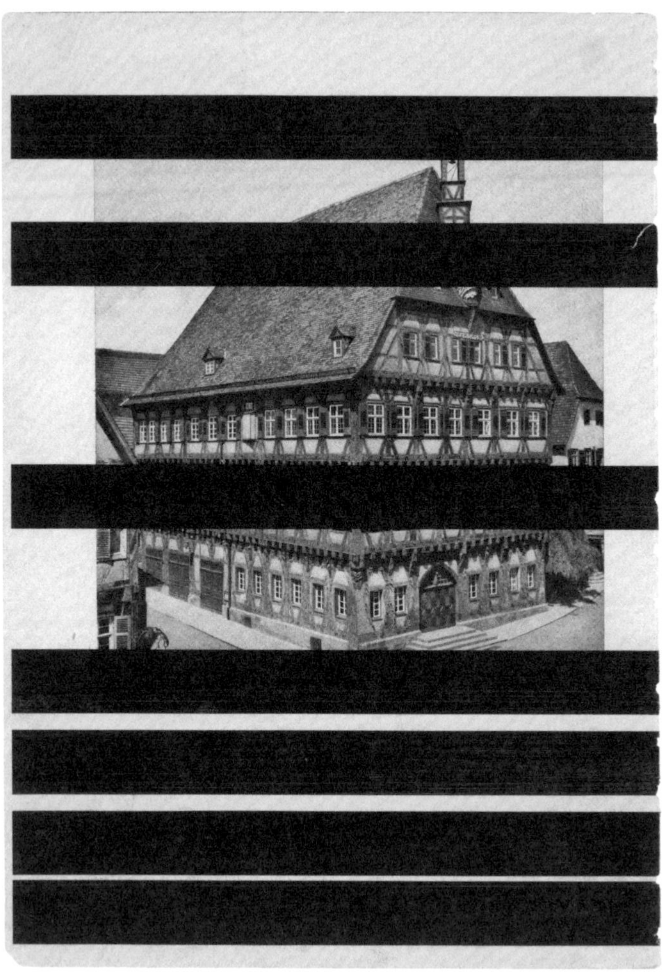

Untitled, 2002
Epson DURABrite inkjet on book page, 26.4 × 18.7 cm

"Tradition … involves, in the first place, the historical sense … a perception, not only of the pastness of the past, but of its presence."
—T.S. Eliot, *Tradition and the Individual Talent*, 1922

With its citations from the history of Modernism, the pastness of the past is as much apparent in Wade Guyton's work as the past's continued presence rearticulated with an awareness of the critical strategies of Postmodernism. Guyton's *Untitled Action Sculpture (Breuer)* (2004) could be seen as an emblematic sculpture. The tubular steel frame of a Marcel Breuer chair is partially un-bent and stretched out to form a tall freestanding abstract sculpture. Enough of its distinctive original shape remains for it to still be recognizable, but its new form implies a random indeterminacy at odds with the structural utilitarianism of its origins. The Modernist fetish object is translated into an essentially useless art object that points toward a tradition of abstraction, but its abstract convictions are troubled by its culturally loaded source material. Its meaning is determinedly open-ended and Guyton's relation to his source remains ambiguous. The iconic object is neither celebrated nor wholly desecrated; the significance of the original remains clear while the deconstructive gesture seems rather to explore the limitations of transformation within the individual's reach.

Guyton's ongoing series of "printer drawings" enact a similar type of low-key intrusion into the graphic evidence of Modernist history. Pages from books showing (mostly) black and white reproductions of key Modernist art works, or sometimes timber frame houses, are fed through a home-office ink jet printer and marked with thick black or red marks, drawn up on a word document. A black rectangle blots out half of a Moholy-Nagy construction; a group of smudged black circles disturb the pleasing geometry of a Kenneth Noland painting; a "U" blown up to an exaggerated scale straddles another image. The overwhelming impulse is to recognize the "true" picture beneath the clumsy surrogate geometries superimposed on it; the tradition beneath the contemporary doodlings. As with the Breuer chair, Guyton leaves this possibility open, merely encumbering his image with traces of more recent artistic activity. While these drawings could be read as reflections on the soft geometry of word processing and Photoshop versus the hardline conceptual geometries of Modernism, or of the readily available technological means of home reproduction versus the limited possibilities of photographic reproduction that first appeared in art books in the mid-20th century, such easy dichotomies are weakened by the ambiguity, and apparent randomness, of the final images. They do not imply a superceding of the past but rather lay it out to suggest its contiguous "presence" and "pastness," as well as the complexities facing a young artist in confronting it. As Eliot first put it [in *Tradition and the Individual Talent*], and the rest of the century confirmed, "no artist of any art, has his complete meaning alone. His significance, his appreciation is the appreciation of his relation of the dead poets and artists."

Ambivalence is a central characteristic of Guyton's work. He makes a point of choosing pages at random to

over-print, or signs with no singular meaning, and is at pains
to avoid an easy elegance. As a result, there is nothing
simple or neat about his works and rather a sense of endgame
whereby narrative is alluded to but not concluded. It is
partially obscured, but thereby all the more present, as John
Baldessari described it: "the point is—the return of the
repressed. The more you try to blot it out, the more it's
going to be there." But his relation to the sources he chooses
remains open-ended, confused by the apparent lack of
intention of his creative decision-making. A circular process
ensues of self-conscious citation overlaid with unsophisti-
cated sign-making, where formal decisions are handed over
to the rather less than perfect technology of the ink-jet
printer, and ensuing smears, blots, and misalignments are
absorbed into the final design. Arranged in series between
panes of glass in heavy wooden frames, the narrative codes
of the art books as much as the textual codes of the computer-
printer process are broken and the works stutter in dumb
looping repetition. The effect is somewhat like Richard
Prince's joke paintings, bad jokes repeated and repeated
until the words themselves seem alienated and meaningless
and humor gives way to an aching melancholy. But Guyton
has described his works as "an act of processing," not
"negation" which results in "stasis" rather than nihilism;
the stasis of tradition perhaps where the past is absorbed
by the present as much as the present is determined by
the past.

The Lights Are Out in The Land of Necessity

Daniel Baumann

Originally published in Yilmaz Dziewior and Janneke de Vries (eds.), *Wade Guyton: Color, Power &*
Style, Walther König, Cologne 2006, p. 111–117.

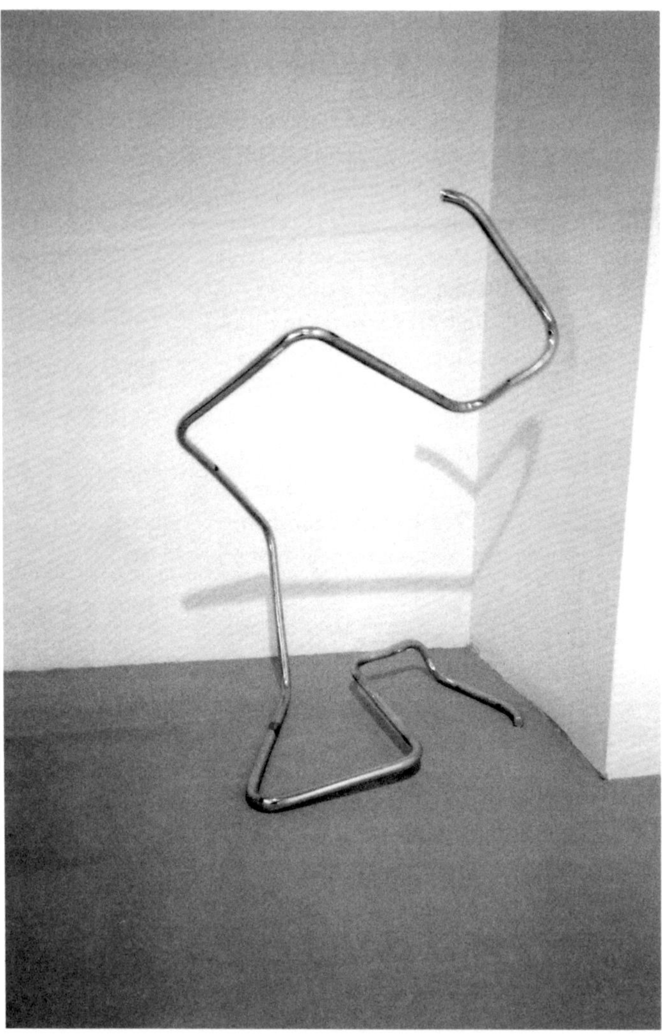

Untitled Action Sculpture (Chair), 2001
Altered steel chair, 119.4 × 86.4 × 81.3 cm

I follow the path the other way
around. Why do we go to galleries
and museums, and look at the art?
Because it is not necessary to do
so. In the same way as there is no
necessity to look up at the blue
sky. About 200 years ago art gradually released itself from the need
to serve religion and feudal power.
It made itself independent and
gradually stopped working on com-
mission. The bourgeoisie came
to power and allocated the role of
freedom to art. They offered it
autonomy, but in exchange wanted
to use it as a screen for projecting
their ideas of independence and
self-determination. While industri-
alization and capitalism were bringing them power and affluence, the
artist represented a lost contrasting
ideal: they created their work on
the basis of a free decision, on the
far side of the division of labor,
and without looking at the market.
Because the artist's life was not
subordinated to a purpose, they
embodied freedom itself.

This apparently self-determined lack of purpose made them the new hero of a society that defined itself through work, time, and economic success. Therefore it is not by chance that busts honoring artists, composers, and writers were set up in parks, the sites of controlled leisure. The history of the avant-garde and Modernism drew an alternative picture, but it was a story of heroism, too. It was based on the belief that the true artist develops his vision from uncompromising necessity and is willing to pay a high price for that purpose, such as incomprehension and rejection. These days it is almost impossible not to share this view; even though the work of Marcel Duchamp, one of the protagonists of this heroic story, resists every kind of necessity. Critics and art historians have punished this attitude with interpretations and discourses, as if it were necessary to justify something. The compulsion toward self-legitimization binds the bourgeoisie to the Modernist and the avant-garde.

In recent years Wade Guyton has made a series of apparently site-specific interventions by using an X-shaped object. Each "X" was made of two long planks, which were painted black and then screwed together into their final form. Once he had completed the "X," the artist set up the drawing-like object in a way that suggested that someone had left a piece of meaning behind. In the Californian desert in 2003 an "X" was leaned against a Joshua tree for the *High Desert Test Sites* project. Within a short time it fell down and since then has been moldering away where it fell. Another stood in an exhibition in Tbilisi, Georgia, in 2004, in the corner of the exhibition hall, as if waiting to be there for something. A third leaned against another artist's sculpture for support (Secession, Vienna 2003), and at the Whitney Biennial 2004 in New York Guyton left his sign under the footbridge of the museum, in a corner, as if it were a discarded prop that would soon be transported somewhere else. In all cases these interventions were adapted to the place; they were never coincidental, but not compulsive either. The object itself was neither a cross nor a letter nor a sculpture nor a picture; it was a sign without a riddle, transparent in its construction and unambiguous in form. Without forcing itself on anyone, the "X" pointed to the possibility of believing in abstraction and function, the possibility of some interest creating meaning for context and autonomy, the need for necessity and interpretation and the inevitability of emptiness and chance.

In an article on Wade Guyton's work, the American art historian Johanna Burton wrote: "They are too easily generalized to be attributed to any singular context and, because of this, are not naturally of any context at all."[1]

While Guyton, with the "X," created a sign without meaning, he took the opposite path by taking apart Marcel Breuer's famous Cesca chair. After removing the seat and back section, he folded the tubular steel frame, with a few simple movements turning an icon of Modernism into an abstract image that might well be called a "sculpture." Laconically, with little external effort, Guyton thus prepares fields of reference that arouse in us, like a reflex, the need to interpret and match his work with a context: Modernism, sculpture, performance, artwork, design, their history, their interrelationships, their status today, and the innumerable discourses about it all. The 20th century was obsessed with a need to accompany art with words and theories. On the other hand, art itself again and again sought an affinity with discourse. And this was not just a matter of clarification and interpretation, but also and always the ennoblement of this discipline, because the visual arts did not have the same status as literature, philosophy, and music. The history of art in the 20th century cannot be separated from its struggle for recognition as an intellectual discipline. And as abstraction grew, its interpretations grew more hysterical.

Another group of works by Wade Guyton presents itself in the form of prints. As with the sculptures, here again the production process is significant, but without wanting to explain anything. With the help of the "drawing" tool on the word-processing application called Word, Guyton produces patterns, manipulating their composition and colors on screen in the simplest way. He then tears illustrated pages out of catalogues and books, inserts them in the inkjet printer and issues the "print" command. The pattern is printed onto the book page, without Guyton testing its position in advance. Brought together into series, the printed pages are arranged within massive wooden frames and hung on the wall. The production method, the inclusion of chance, the combination of various materials and techniques, the obvious manipulation of motifs, the elegance of the aesthetics employed, the staged presentation, the interest in art history and its discourses and playing with different expectations bring about interpretive gaps, which we have not only learned to recognize but which we are willing to fill in.

If we refuse this invitation to interpret, our escape route is work-centered observation. For that reason I would now have to say that the works on canvas, which Guyton has been producing since 2005, continue the principle of the printed book pages, or rather adapt them to the painting medium. With the help of the computer, Guyton produces abstract motifs on the screen and then prints them out on linen with an inkjet printer. Here again the result cannot be foreseen, because the technique causes errors again and again, for example injecting too much ink so that it drips. The results are abstract pictures. Some look like beach towels, others are painterly-picturesque, yet others are formally perfect or can be allocated a place in the history of abstract painting.

The following can be said of the U-shaped sculptures of polished steel: they have been around in various sizes since 2004 and they extend the U-motif from the prints into three-dimensions. They also offer a wide range of reference points. They are, as Umberto Eco would say, "open" art-works, so that many interpretations can offer a meaning: ashtray, paperweight, Constantin Brancusi, the rediscovery of sculpture by the younger generation of artists, the dream of autonomy, belief in form, Max Bill, Ikea, design, appropriation, nostalgia, Bauhaus, post-conceptualism.

No, there is no reason to be desperate. Rhetorically Guyton's works function in such a way that their elegance, openness, and multiplicity of reference suggest interpre-tations that are relativist and empty rather than meaningful. And so we, the viewers, lose our task and our legitimacy. For beyond all revolutions of form and content, which art has passed through since Impressionism, still today the most remote artworks bond with each other through their demand for an active recipient. Even the Impressionists were convinced that painting reaches perfection only in the eye of the beholder. The readymade then replaced the retina with the brain. The concept of an active viewer, who takes responsibility for their seeing, corresponded to the ideal of

a mature and educated citizen demanded by democratic
bourgeois society. All that no longer seems to work. That
is the only thing I understand when I stand in front of
Wade Guyton's works. They make me desperate. They make
me joyful.

[1] See Johanna Burton, "Such Uneventful Events: The Work
of Wade Guyton," here p. 30–35. Also of interest is her
article "How Does the Verb Work When One Speaks of
Collaboration? On Recent Work by Wade Guyton and
Kelley Walker." It appeared in 2005 in the catalogue
Guyton/Walker: The Failever of Judgement, JRP|Ringier,
Zurich 2005.

Modern Pictures
Scott Rothkopf

Originally published in Yilmaz Dziewior and Janneke de Vries (eds.), *Wade Guyton: Color, Power &* *Style*, Walther König, Cologne 2006, p. 64–83.

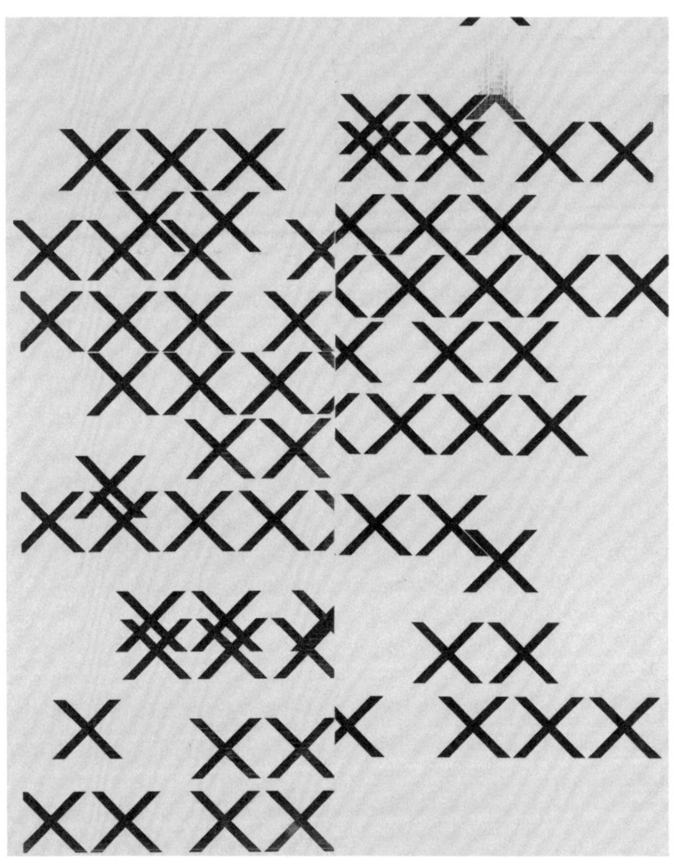

Untitled, 2006
Epson UltraChrome inkjet on linen, 216.5 × 175.3 cm

Painting Lessons

It is the summer of 2004, and Wade Guyton is, improbably, making paintings. "Improbably," I admit, may be something of a cover for my own bafflement on first encountering the color-infused linen panels that were tacked all over his studio walls like a Constructivist's dorm room, but it is safe to say that nothing in the artist's career thus far had portended a turn to that most privileged and problematic of mediums. Guyton had, after all, occupied himself until then almost entirely with minimal sculptures and small drawings made on his desktop printer by marking letters and shapes on the pages of old art books, usually bearing images from modernism's past. But here was a room full of colorful *paintings*, or at least works on canvas—a support that for artists from Richard Tuttle to Blinky Palermo had come to signify the medium as much, if not more, than paint itself. When asked

how he had decided to take the plunge into the deep end
of the artistic gene pool, Guyton described his impetus with
characteristically measured nonchalance: scraps of brown
linen were lying around the studio he shared with the painter
Judith Eisler, and thinking about his "printer drawings,"
he wondered, "If I call these things drawings, how would I
make a painting?" Not very differently, it turns out.

Guyton began by cutting strips of unprimed linen
down to a width that could fit through his desktop printer and
proceeded to mark them with his standard "U"s and circles,
often running the material through the machine multiple
times, as he had with some of his drawings. This additive process was not simply a fallback compositional strategy, but
became newly necessary—given that the printer could only
cover an area of certain height—if the paintings were to
approach the grander scale that has traditionally distinguished
the medium from drawing. By marking each end of the
canvas on a different side, Guyton could then fold over the
top portion of the linen once it was mounted to the wall,
effectively doubling the vertical area he could cover with ink.
None of this was rocket science, of course, and the results
feel a bit unresolved, something Guyton may have tacitly
acknowledged by never letting them out of his studio. Yet
these tentative experiments in painting contained one crucial,
if fleeting, innovation: the addition of scanned images to
his limited lexicon of marks. There, amid the typed "U"s and
rendered rectangles, appear a picture of a triangular wooden
bracket placed directly on a flatbed scanner, and a pattern
of alternating green and red bars taken from the inside cover
of a dismembered book. At first, one might not even notice
that these printed signs are of an entirely, different order than
both those that surround them and all of the others that had
heretofore populated Guyton's art. But the wooden bracket
betrays a slight sense of three-dimensional modeling, just as
the green and red stripes seem more perfectly parallel and
evenly spaced than the shapes and patterns he usually dashed
off onscreen. Having abandoned the resistant ground of
his drawings' printed book pages, Guyton may have instinctively reached for an *image* to introduce onto the tabula rasa
of the blank canvas—anything, that is, to keep the new
paintings from being purely formal compositions of abstracts
elements, which is precisely what they became.

Not fully aware of the implications of his scanned images, Guyton set them aside and began work on the paintings I encountered in his studio a few months later. The purchase of an Epson commercial inkjet printer had allowed the canvases to reach some 44-inches in width, and they bore rickety grids, shapes, and "U"s in Guyton's familiar red and black and the quite unfamiliar orange, green, and cerulean blue. Like their slimmer predecessors, the new canvases had passed through the printer multiple times, something particularly evident in the transparent layering of colors and perhaps even more so in the nagging sense that no artist—no matter how untrained in the rudiments of design—could bring himself consciously to create compositions quite so gauche. This awkwardness, though, turned out to be the paintings' interest, a strangely convincing index of Guyton's process, which, whether by accident or cosmic design, had landed him squarely between the Bauhaus abstractions and unprimed Color Field canvases that constitute two of his recurring art historical predilections. Yet even at their best, the products of Guyton's first foray into painting seemed to be missing something, their wheels spinning but failing to find real traction in the universe of reproductions that had always served as the bedrock of his art. They would prove a remarkably generative dead end on a path toward a new kind of painting—one that would suspend his drawings' dichotomous structure between artistic reproduction and supplemental mark; one that could function both abstractly *and* as an image; one, above all, that could speak to layered histories and yet engage unequivocally the image culture of our time.

The Rules of the Game

As his first tentative experiments in painting suggest, Guyton's practice proceeds according to a fairly narrow set of guidelines that roughly delimit the decisions and actions he will or will not allow himself in creating a work of art. From his student days, he recalls, he never had a particular interest in *making* things, his initial attraction to the field being the heady post-Duchampian proposition that to join the ranks of artists one need do almost nothing at all. Without a manual skill set, he veered—whether by inclination or practical exigency—toward deceptively simple structures or appropriations, such as refabricating a suddenly vanished, generic Minimal sculpture that he had passed daily on his walk to work through New York's Madison Square Park. His studio, like that of many artists of his generation, was really more of a quasi-office—the virtual and physical desktop acting as an arena for a kind of ambling conceptual activity. Appropriately enough, Guyton's first drawings were almost doodles: blacking out the photographed silhouette of a modern suburban manse; marking a window in a picture of the Farnsworth House with what would become his trademark "X." So suspicious was he toward any kind of obvious creative expenditure that even that most minimal of gestures inspired a near existentialist crisis. "Why am I making this drawing?" he recalls asking himself. "It seemed dumb to be sitting here drawing, but it didn't seem dumb enough. If I was going to do something that required no skill, it shouldn't require my labor." And soon thereafter it did not.

Perched at his desk, Guyton experienced a modest eureka moment. "My printer was sitting there," he recalls, "and it just seemed like a more efficient way to make this mark." He opened Microsoft Word; typed an "X" in Blair ITC Medium (a sans serif font that felt as blandly modern as his favored iconography); and printed it on top of a catalogue page. This simple action inaugurated a working method that persists to this day, a way of making drawings without really drawing, a way of taking something from the past and just barely making it his own. To his "X"s, Guyton would sparingly add "U"s, circles, rectangles, and sometimes combinations thereof, all created simply in word-processing software and printed atop catalogue pages charting an expansive taxonomy of modernist abstraction in its most vaunted and debased forms (Guyton was not particularly aware of the difference, he claims, when he began to learn about art). From the start, his serial technique relied on a kind of Johnsian approach to variation and recycling and on chance as a motor to generate compositions and pictorial incident that he seemed afraid—or simply unwilling—to take responsibility for himself. Although he may plan an arrangement of shapes on the screen with a certain catalogue page in mind, he can never really know how it will land on the paper until after he hits print. If things seem to be getting a bit too arty, he may apply the same Word file over and over again to a variety of book pages, sometimes jamming them in the machine one on top of another so they receive the printed pattern in random interlaced fragments. From its inception, then, Guyton's system introduced a tension between conception (of you could properly call it that) and execution—a dynamic triangulation between his own very limited decision making, his chosen technology, and the manifestation of their interaction in the world.

Within this artistic matrix, decision is at once cheapened and deferred, yet paradoxically made to seem more weighty in the parsimony with which Guyton metes it out. Manual and intellectual labor are expended only when required: the strength necessary to bend this Breuer chair, the decisiveness needed to color that circle red. But why such hesitation? Why any strictures at all? This is a question that would dog me when thinking about Guyton's drawings and, later, about the printed paintings that would come to involve just three basic motifs over some 15 months. "Go ahead, type a 'Z,'" I wanted to tell him. "Add a triangle to your repertoire of shapes." I could understand why Ellsworth Kelly, with Picasso at his back in Paris in 1948, needed chance or grids not to compose; or why Frank Stella, in the shadow of de Kooning, pioneered "deductive structures." But is not Guyton's privilege—and that of his generation—to be working at a time when no artistic position seems out of bounds, no varnished nude or cubic construction too capricious an undertaking? What was the point—apart from an air of asceticism or an utter lack of imagination—in using only two letters in twice as many years?

The problem, of course, is that within this vast field of possibility it is hard to find a set of urgent parameters, a wall to push against, an artistic father on which to enact our Oedipal scenarios. How far back would we have to look to find this resistance? To a time, perhaps, when there were critical strictures that both guided a practice and begged to be broken. Indeed, the yearning may have something to do with the recurring fascination among young artists today, Guyton included, with modernism's optimistic early convictions and its diabolical late dogma, as well as with those figures of the 1960s and 1970s who laid them to waste.

You could call it nostalgia, or you could call it common sense. But whether one takes such backward glances as a negative emotional symptom or a pragmatic search for a discursive toehold, they ultimately speak less to the certainties of the past than the bewilderment of the present. At a time when anything is possible, Guyton, like many artists before him, has chosen to play with a very small deck of cards. His thematic and procedural strictures might be seen as an attempt simply to keep making work, while creating structural parameters in which purposeful variation and accident can take on new meaning—or any meaning at all. "Rules are necessary," as he puts it "because otherwise everything remains arbitrary, and then how do you continue? If everything is arbitrary there can be no interaction or manipulation of the system." There is something touching in all this, in the endless rows of "X"s, in the curious questioning of what this bar of color might do to that ground, in knowing that you cannot just type a "Z." One beauty—and potential pathos—of Guyton's method is his very questioning of how one might convincingly impose limits on a practice at a time when there would otherwise seem to be none.

German Lessons

Guyton first exhibited his new paintings in Yilmaz Dziewior's *Formalism. Modern Art, Today* at the Kunstverein in Hamburg in 2004, where he experienced something of an epiphany. There his linen pieces shared space with the paintings and sculpture of Martin Boyce, Sergej Jensen, Stefan Müller, Anselm Reyle, and Katja Strunz, among other artists reinvestigating the potential—and pitfalls—of formal abstraction. Guyton would seem a natural fit with this company, given that the book pages on which he makes his drawings frequently feature modernism's fathers (or twice-removed cousins), and the sparse letters and shapes he adds to them allude to that tradition's favored forms. His paintings, meanwhile, seemed headed only more directly into that historical stream. Indeed, with good reason, many viewers and critics of Guyton's work have simply assumed that it is *about* modernism, if not precisely *of* it.

Yet if his canvases felt at home in this context, Guyton, perhaps to his own surprise, did not. As he recalls, "I wasn't

really sure about the work's relationship to his whole group
of artists involved with a return to Constructivism and
earlier abstraction. Seeing the show, I understood what their
interests were and realized that these weren't my interests.
I thought there was a kind a romanticism of style in much
of the work, and my raw linen, too, had a particular connotation." So while Guyton may have work starring Gabo or
Albers, Noland or Stella, he was not attempting to revivify
or advance a particular lineage of abstraction, as Reyle
or Strunz, no matter how resourcefully and self-consciously,
may be. His work, in fact, owes far more to an altogether
different paterfamilias, one rarely acknowledged directly
within its expansive image bank, yet absolutely palpable
in its appropriative strategies and sometimes stagy air. These
are artists who (for better, worse, or pure convenience) are
grouped under the banner of "postmodernism," figures like
Louise Lawler, Richard Prince, Cindy Sherman, and Jeff
Wall from who Guyton inherited—if not a particular style
or working method—an all-consuming world view. "That's
the art I learned how to make art from," he has remarked.
"I didn't learn from reading about Gabo; I learned from
Jeff Wall. That work is clearly more important to me than
any abstract painting." After his Hamburg experience,
Guyton acknowledged as much by slipping individual Wall
and Sherman reproductions into his drawings in a sly riposte
to his misinterpreters. But if he were to continue making
paintings—or any art, for that matter—he would need a
sustainable way to make this frame of reference clear, a way,
that is, to fold it into his practice, but not through his
drawings' literal quotation alone. What the paintings needed,
as he put it, "was another image to play around with."
He needed a *picture*.

Wade Guyton Paints a Picture

Guyton's second foray into painting can be understood as a
direct response to the first, a way of working through the
misgivings and insights of his Hamburg experience. To begin,
he dispensed with the raw canvas so ripe with "romantic
connotations" and ordered wooden stretchers and bolts of
high quality linen primed with lead white. As long as he was
making "paintings," he seemed to suggest, he might as well

go all the way and find a ground that could set off his marks rather than absorbing them into a cohesive whole. The first few canvases of this second campaign found him grasping for the "image" that he must have instinctively felt missing from the previous abstractions. He began by printing a length of canvas with a composition of a red rectangle surmounted by a black circle, which he had used in a number of drawings. Here was a preexisting image file, but one that hardly attested to its prior status as a "picture" and ended up looking more *école de* Malevich than gang of Prince. Another attempt involved a blown-up scan of an inverted, umlaut-crowned "ö" (cut from the word "Köln") but it, too, hardly spoke to a prior life outside the canvas. Guyton, of course, could have turned to any of the myriad photographic sources that filled his studio (and in one case even did so), but he must have sensed he needed a sign that could operate at once as an image *and* as an abstract element that could be co-opted and redeployed without getting bogged down in specific references or subject matter. The answer to this dilemma, it turned out, was right beneath his nose. He found it in the unassuming pattern of green and red stripes that had appeared and then unceremoniously vanished from his earliest linen strips.

Once enlarged and printed on primed canvas, Guyton's parallel bands came alive with a previously unforeseen semantic and pictorial elasticity. Unlike the raw linen, the hard white ground could register fine detail and thereby exploit those photo-reproductive capabilities that have made inkjet printers beloved by just about everybody with a digital camera. Guyton, though, had never capitalized on this potential, always printing flat shapes and letters as a foil for his photographically charged grounds. The stripes, at first, would seem to be no different from those earlier shapes: flat, abstract, essentially scaleless, requiring no skill, their banal Christmas colors vaguely even "dumb." But when printed 44-inches across (the maximum width allowed by his printer) the image betrays a trace of trompe l'oeil illusionism along its upper border. There, the stripes terminate in a frayed edge that, though perfectly flat, appears to push ever so slightly off the canvas. Even if we are unaware that the pattern comes from the inside covers of a paperback book, the uneven tear subtly announces it as a design—indeed, as a physical *thing*—not of Guyton's creation but literally ripped from the graphic and material stuff of the world. These are stripes but also, the torn edge reminds us, a picture of stripes, and the reciprocities and distinctions between the two hits at the very core of his art.

Guyton's rediscovery of his modest device unleashed a torrent of ideas and activity. As with his earlier drawings, he immediately seized on a serial method, testing variation after variation on his new motif. While the width of the paintings was essentially determined by that of his printer, when stretching his canvases he varied both their height and the disposition of the graphic within them. He determined that the stripes would always run edge to edge, but a white margin would appear above and sometimes below them. This arrangement accomplished two things: first, by laterally filling the painting, the pattern flattened the pictorial field and obviated Guyton's earlier difficulties with manipulating a figure on a ground; yet, second, by maintaining a margin above or beneath the stripes, Guyton could simultaneously bracket his device as an "imported," preexisting image (just has the margins of the printed page had always been a crucial component of his drawings). These two, somewhat opposed, strategies establish a dynamic tension within the works, causing us always to vacillate between reading each painting as an integral allover field or a cut-and-paste collage, between an abstract composition and a kind of readymade representation. When left completely bare, the upper areas often feel uncomfortably empty. Too big properly to be called "margins," the inert white rectangles open onto a strange distinction between negative space and blank space: the former being that compositionally active bit of ground that has played a key role in the development of modern painting since Cézanne, the latter more evocative of our contemporary pasteup universe, the eerie residue of a potentially boundless space framed within a computer window's scroll bars.

Guyton often imparts this dead zone with floating black circles, sometimes framed by faint haloes of parallel skid marks that lend them an ambiguous velocity. As foils for the colorful pattern below, they again posit the slippery distinction between an abstraction and a "picture," since they are not scanned images but geometrical figures "drawn" on the computer (yet unlike a freehand scrawl, they rely on a preexisting formula that makes them both an abstraction and a kind of nameable, conventional sign). Hovering in theether above the stripes they look for all the world like the 21st-century bastard progeny of Adolph Gottlieb. It is not surprising, of course, that Guyton's new formal vocabulary would hark back to earlier episodes of modernism in both major and minor keys—whether the stripes of Gene Davis, Daniel Buren, and Frank Stella, or the buoyant orbs of the Constructivists and Alexander Liberman, artists who in some cases had already appeared in Guyton's corpus. The difference here is that he has succeeded in summoning all of these predecessors and more without a single specific reference. Instead, the allusions operate with a lightness of touch that allows us to see them as but one element at play in a larger circuit of artistic activity and meaning.

Pictures Puzzles

If Guyton's relationship to modernism demanded a more modulated inflection, his hold on an altogether different set of artistic precepts would prove no less problematic. Here I am referring to the critical apparatus launched by Douglas Crimp in his seminal 1977 exhibition and essay *Pictures*, which couched the return to representation in the art of the late 1970s "not in the familiar guise of realism, which seeks to resemble a prior existence, but as an autonomous function that might be described as 'representation as such.'" Crimp's profound thinking, and the art it came to frame, whether by Jack Goldstein or Sherrie Levine, Richard Prince or Cindy Sherman, is now so deeply hardwired in the artistic consciousness that it need not be rehearsed here. Indeed, for artists and critics of Guyton's (and my) generation—one for which there was no "Life Before Pictures"— the concept of a world made up of representations *en abîme* seems so natural as to be taken less as received wisdom than self-evident fact. So persistent is this condition that it has given rise to a new kind of artistic double bind or even stutter: the circumstances of image circulation hardly need to be restated, but failure to at least wink or nod in their direction implies some kind of reactionary will to an innocence we never quite hard. The real problem—and here is where an older generation may have had its cake and eaten it too—it is not so much saying there is no such thing as an original image, but knowing full well that it is not a very original thing to say.

This nagging dilemma is one to which Guyton's work is implicitly addressed. We are late not just to modernism's party, but to postmodernism's, too. How, then, to figure this belatedness, to acknowledge a particular historicity while also charting a path forward? Guyton's answer, in part, had been to cross the wires, to subject modernist iconography to the artistic strategies that superseded it, all the while leaving traces of both in plain view. As opposed to Prince (who effaced the Marlboro logo from his rephotographed cowboys) or Levine (who seamlessly integrated her source material into her own output), Guyton, like his sometime collaborator Kelley Walker, always insists on leaving the apparatus of citation glaringly intact. In his drawings, we find not just poached images but yawning margins, torn bindings, page numbers, plate numbers, and captions—all details that speak to the process of quotation before Guyton's stab at it has ever begun. Layers of art history are superimposed not via a panoply of style but through transpositions of image and method, source and approach. The final veneers are unmistakably of our epoch: printed marks everyone knows from the home office and, even more telling, a choice of imagery that reveals a "period eye" guided by a canny sense of today's most *recherché* retro-chic.

Nevertheless, now that appropriationnist strategies practically constitute a new "natural" state, what is being borrowed tends to take precedence over how it is done. Following this logic, it is not surprising that Guyton's work has often been read primarily in terms of its relationship to modernism, its subjects more than its means. In his first raw linen paintings, he may have in fact been trying to escape the potential stranglehold of such garrulous iconography. Writing on these works, critic Johanna Burton astutely observed that he had grown wary of the "contentment of content," the fact that "appropriated images … sometimes risk slipping into representational roll call." Yet "pure form," as we have seen, posed the inverse peril, acting too much like an earnest abstraction rather than as a "picture" in quotation marks. Guyton's first striped paintings were a way out of this corner, and in the works that followed, he would further refine—or better, confuse—the tenuous rapprochement between his various frames of reference, summoning modernism's representatives not as a referential end in themselves but as a means through which to explore the complicated realities of picture making today.

Inky Depths

Emboldened by his success with the stripes, Guyton soon sought to introduce a new image to his repertoire, one, as he put it, that might be "even more picturely" than the first. For years he had been collecting various editions of Stephen King's *Firestarter* (1980), and he found a different book with flames on its cover, which he eventually threw on the scanner after blacking out its title with marker. The resultant image was certainly "more picturely" than anything Guyton had printed thus far: a solid black rectangle with yellow flames erupting along its base, it was far less timid about its status as an image—and, in fact, as an image *of* an image—than the largely abstract stripes. Guyton, however, was more cautious, adding it to several book pages and even printing it alone on an unstretched piece of linen, before finally testing it in his paintings (in a wry homage to Yves Klein's torched canvases). He first used the scan as a background on which he superimposed a group of ten overlapping "U"s in yellow, orange, purple, blue, green, and red. Seeing the painting exhibited in New York last summer, I was nearly as perplexed by it as I was by the linen pieces a year before. Compared to Guyton's ordinarily restrained palette and composition, it seemed almost baroque. The image runs edge to edge on the canvas, which is so loaded with ink that the contours of the letters are overwhelmed with blurry drips that make them appear as if they are literally dissolving into a lush inky stream. This unprecedented painterliness is matched by a beguiling narrative charge that is at once ominous and slightly hokey. We are not really sure what the "U"s are doing in the fire, apart from serving as the hapless subjects on which Guyton can exact his painterly experiments. But this narrative ambiguity itself shows him trying to come to terms with the full range of meaning that a *picture* might allow.

Guyton, it turns out, may have been as puzzled as I was, because the subsequent canvases represent something of a clarifying retreat. The fire remained, but the "U"s now appeared no more than three to a canvas, which necessarily restricted both the compositional variables and the number of colors he had to choose. A more difficult problem may have been that the image, when run full bleed, implied a kind of atmospheric depth that operated less as a picture than a picture window, thereby undermining the stripe paintings' masterful suspension of precisely those terms. Once again, Guyton's solution lay at the edges of the image, which he proceeded to print and stretch so as to include details inadvertently caught by the scanner: the tattered top edge of the original dust jacket, a thin portion of the book cover beneath it, and a whitish crease running down the painting's left side where the book's binding would be. Now, if one were tempted to enter the canvas' fiery depths, a glance toward the layered trompe l'oeil detail at the periphery would push the picture plane forward, blunting the illusion—or at least supplanting it with another one. Perhaps more importantly, these details reconnected the image to its source in printed matter, an origin subtly underscored by the texture of the blown-up flames, which reveal the dot screen of their original commercial printing. There is something almost quaint about this meta-thread in Guyton's work, which suggests an attachment to printed matter at a time when just about any generic jpeg can be plucked from the Internet. Yet this attention to the flames' prior support plays an important role in his twisted chain of reference, marking a previous stage in the life of an image as it shuttles among various physical incarnations, and dips in and out of the digital ether.

Indeed, Guyton's growing investigation of the digital realm and its relationship to our physical one constitutes one of the key fascinations of his recent paintings. Here, it should be said, however, that he has scarcely more mastery of Photoshop than oil painting, and his work shares none of the technophilia evident in so much contemporary art. To the contrary, he approaches the computer in a decidedly offhand fashion, similar to the way artists like Ed Ruscha picked up the point-and-shoot camera in the 1960s. In Guyton's hands, typing, scanning, basic image manipulation, and inkjet printing constitute nothing less than a new vernacular. But nothing more than one either. He wields his tools with more pragmatism than finesse, knowing better than to over-invest them with a futuristic glamour that can only ever be fleeting. Like the various obsolete photo-reproductive processes catalogued in his book pages, the paintings, too, embody a technological moment that will inevitably pass (something Guyton acknowledges by including the brand name and specific type of ink used in his lists of materials). That moment, of course, is today, and one of the things that makes his paintings so contemporary—perhaps in contradistinction to those of many other young "formalists"—is their inquisitive and deeply felt grappling with our immediate technological landscape.

Accidents Happen

As Guyton's first New York solo exhibition approached last spring, he knew that he wanted to show paintings, and he knew that they needed to be big. The new gallery where they were to be hung felt smaller than he had expected, and his answer, as it is often the case, was to try and make the work feel a little "wrong," too large and too much for the space. This was easier said than done, though, since, as we have seen, his printer's capabilities had determined the maximum width of his paintings from the start. His answer proved as low-tech as they tend to be, harking back to the doubled-over structures of his earliest linen strips: by folding a double-width canvas in two and taping together its edges, as he had done a few times in his drawings, he could print half the image on one side and then flip it over and feed the material through again.

I remember visiting Guyton's studio shortly after the first few canvases of this kind were completed. A large fire painting looked glamorous, but somehow simply bigger than the last, making nothing critical of its newfound heft. On another wall hung the first painting ever to employ Guyton's signature "X," a cameo appearance perhaps encouraged by the obvious play between the letter's bilateral symmetry and the vertical crease created from folding the canvas in two. Over 50 "X"s march across its surface in uneven overlapping rows, which are slightly out of vertical alignment on either side of the central seam. This accident was the product of

Guyton's difficulty in starting to print each side at exactly the same point, since the machine draws in the fabric until its optical sensor determines a proper place to begin discharging ink. Slightly more disconcerting, though, is the fact that a narrow strip of the image appears to have disappeared into the crease, which creates the off-kilter feeling of the picture being pinched from behind or made up of two overlapping planes. The image file was clearly scaled too big for the canvas, and rather than trimming the excess off the edges, Guyton may have mistakenly cropped a strip out of the middle when dividing it onscreen for printing. Looking at the painting, there is a sense that something has been lost, but also that something has been gained. And what is gained, perhaps, is the very awareness of what has been lost. For this unnerving Rorschach, more than any of Guyton's paintings before it, gives elegant and economical form to that unstable projective link between a digital image and its physical manifestation, between the idea of an artwork and what it actually becomes. A fold in space, the painting tells us, is not some sci-fi fantasy or elaborate computer model, but a simple fuck-up in properly getting an image onto its ground—a disconnect that refashions the age old interface between mind and hand for our computer age.

Guyton's chance discovery pointed a way to make his new paintings' central seam—and thereby their doubled size—a self-conscious, even poignant, device in the work. As he has remarked, "I've become interested in when something starts as an accident and then becomes a template for other things, or reproduces itself and generates its own logic until something else intervenes to change it." Armed with his new understanding of the paintings' bifurcated structure, Guyton was able to reprise the fire motif to new effect. In one example featuring a trio of letters, the left side of the painting is flawlessly executed, a pale turquoise "U" standing crisply against its ground. But something clearly went awry when printing the second side. The left edge of a white "U" is just barely sliced off by the central seam, and while the two sides of the letter meet at its top, they fall completely out of the synch at its base, a glitch mirrored in the truncated form of a red "U" hovering above. It is as though the canvas got delayed on its way through the printer, its movement failing to keep pace with the visual information it was to receive.

Below the "U"s, things really fall apart: a horizontal white slit pierces through the ground like a peek through a Venetian blind, and the remaining portion of canvas clearly progressed though the printer at a slight angle, a journey evidenced in the oblique tilt of the fire's misaligned base. If Guyton's fiery background had once appeared to open onto some kind of illusionistic space, here the filmy image suffers a strange violence in keeping with its motif. It slides in pieces across the surface completely unmoored from its ground, which asserts itself through every printing error and even literally as a figure, in the case of the white "U." Meanwhile, the scarlet letter bleeds into the black and is riddled with pure magenta striations where the printer heads—whether jammed, confused, or nearing some kind of mechanical exhaustion—failed to overlay the yellow needed in the CMYK process to make red. If my description sounds vaguely anthropomorphizing, it is because Guyton—without daubing ink to canvas—improbably endows these mechanicals pictures with a lived sense of someone groping his way through the process of bringing an artwork into being. Loss, failure, fragility, and the strain—or frisson—of mismatched temporalities have always figured in his drawings, but in paintings like these, he manages to conjure a completely unsentimental emotional energy from the most impersonal of imagery and technological means.

Clearly, there is a kind of pictorial and narrative extravagance in these works that might make an otherwise conceptually minded artist like Guyton blush. He has become, if not exactly a *painter*, a skillful maker of things that derive a kind of inner necessity from the porous contours of his system. He has learned when the addition of a few extra layers of flame may impart the right dramatic effect; which colors are likely to bleed into each other; when overprinting an image will lend it a luxurious velvety texture; and even how the slightest difference in the quality of a ground will encourage or hinder his telltale drips. Guyton's large new paintings exude a kind of haphazard grandeur, the result of a constant negotiation between technical failure and mastery, physical accident and control. Indeed, some-times it is difficult to tell the difference, as he freely admits to making "accidents" happen when they might serve his ends. If the printer begins the second half of a painting out

of alignment with the first, he might pull on the canvas to
bring it back into line—a correction that can only ever
be accompanied by an error of a different sort. The image
of the artist tugging at his paintings or helping them fold
on top of themselves as they reach the floor only to suffer
from a new smear or scar calls to mind a 21st-century action
painting potentially at odds with its mid-tech means.
But the interaction between the digital and the manual,
the pictorial and the haptic, have always been at the heart
of Guyton's practice and its deeply tooted connection
to the ways in which we haltingly navigate the visual and
technological barrage of our time.

Nowhere is this searching more potently figured than
in Guyton's material juxtapositions of various types of digital
information. In some of his fire paintings, for example, he
inserts black "U"s on top of his black backgrounds. At first,
we only detect their stealthy presence where they happen
to cross over and block out more colorful parts of the composition. But once we grasp their hidden contours, we detect
a slight difference in their hue, since the printer renders
them with pure black ink, while the background black of the
scanned image is composed of various overlaid colors that
sometimes lend it a slight greenish or yellowish cast (ironically, though, this composite "picture" of black can feel
even blacker than its less densely applied, purebred neighbor,
especially in the hovering dark cloud where Guyton marked
out the book's title). Such discrepancies are also evident
when comparing the multiple paintings that feature a Swiss-
cheese-like motif of white circles punched from a dark
ground. In some, the "pure" black background is simply
selected from the computer's palette, while in others Guyton
has made the background out of a cropped detail of the
scanned book cover (a game he gives away by leaving visible
the faintest wisp of flame). Black, then, and not quite black—
though it is difficult to say with certainty which is which.
The most perverse twist comes in Guyton's painting of the
"X"s, the bulk of which originated from a scan of earlier
drawings to which he added others typed directly in Photoshop. The difference between them is almost imperceptible
except that those imported and blown-up from the page
reveal a tinge of yellow along their slightly serrated edges,
while those appended directly on the computer have

perfectly smooth contours and are printed in "pure" black, not a composite approximation of it.

Such juxtapositions recall the distinction between the red and green stripes and their accompanying circles, but the difference between an "X" and a picture of an "X" or black and its "representation" gets into a slightly weirder headspace—and this may be precisely where Guyton means to put us. Here, indeed, is where the wires really get crossed. On the one hand, he seems to be testing both our perceptual acuity and the limits of his new "medium," two inquiries that served as pillars of modernism and call to mind the likes of Mondrian and Malevich, Reinhardt and Ryman. Guided in equal measure by his self-imposed rules, restless intuition, and happenstance, Guyton has developed a formal syntax that advances through the manipulation of its limited variables. But this searching is filtered through the lessons of the Pictures generation, even if its results invite a kind of slow unraveling and close looking ordinarily more associated with a painting than a picture. Each object is a palimpsest of tangled representations, a vessel of indeterminate information. Guyton's paintings, then, seem to resolve his drawings' dialectic between modernist imagery and postmodernist means, if such a distinction could ever really be maintained. The fact of the matter, of course, is that it cannot be, as the uneasy synthesis of his paintings makes plain.

The point, Guyton insists, is not to go out and *say* something about modernism, to mark it, or cancel it, or do any of the things that his work is often presumed to do. That just puts the quotation marks in the wrong place. Rather, he suggests, one can *make* something of this contested heritage, something that does not feel reactionary but rather right now. The difference between two blacks or some stripes and a circle is not merely a matter of old-fashioned connoisseurship, but can be made to describe a kind of lived experience. If there is to be life for painting, Guyton contends, our life must be within it, which is not to say anything about pop culture or autobiography or, for that matter, depiction. And if there is to be life after Pictures, it must be lived with an even greater skepticism toward how an image both comes into being and operates once it has. Never illustrative, Guyton's paintings speak to an everyday

screen culture of scanners and scroll bars, layered windows
that slip in and out of view, thresholds of information that
only reveal themselves when the jpeg loses focus, the printer
falters, or the "X" gets a jagged edge. Technical failure is
aestheticized, but not romanticized. We do the best with
what we have.

Decapitalism
John Kelsey

Originally published in *Rich Texts: Selected Writing for Art*, Daniel Birnbaum and Isabelle Graw (ed.), Institut für Kunstkritik, Hochschule für Bildende Künste, Städelschule, Frankfurt am Main/ Sternberg Press, Berlin 2010, p. 65–74. This essay was intended for a catalogue accompanying the 2006 exhibition *Guyton, Price, Walker, Smith* at Kunsthalle Zürich, Zurich. As the volume was never published, this essay finally appeared in a 2008 "reproduction" of the catalogue printed by 38th Street Publishers, New York.

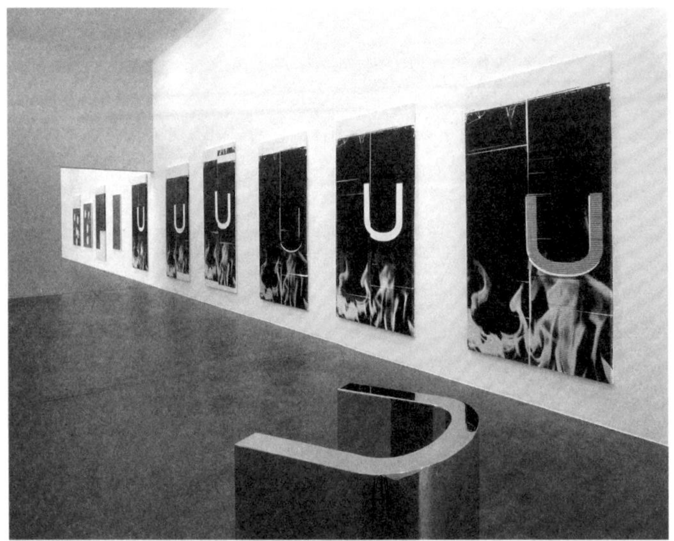

View of the exhibition *Guyton, Price, Smith, Walker*, Kunsthalle Zürich, Zurich, 2006

In the poster for a recent Fra Angelico exhibition at the Metropolitan Museum of Art (2005–2006), saints are being decapitated. They are kneeling in a circle, the sword follows this circle, and blood is gushing from the open holes of their necks. It is remarkable that, even chopped off, the heads keep their golden halos. The bystanders and kings on the left side of the composition seem to notice this too, but it is too late. The heads are like gold coins rolling in the painting, like presidents' heads on money. And is money not like a severed head? It is a sort of decapitation that moves money and everything else with it, as if in a trance. It was Marx who said that meditating on money makes men lose their heads.[1]

Showing together in Europe now for the second time, the artists Wade Guyton, Seth Price, Josh Smith, and Kelley Walker may not be the New Yorkiest band in the world, but if they were, this would be their second album. Let us call them fellow travelers and assume their grouping is at least partly a European construction. It is their packaging and touring as *Guyton, Price, Walker, Smith* (2006) that allows for the production of something like a New York moment in the Kunsthalle, or wherever such moments are in demand. And it could be that the objects and images on view here are not so much things for the eyes, as different ways of entering and inflecting the movement of this entranced circulation. The works themselves seem fascinated by what is happening to them.

If these four artists were a group, *The Decapitation of Saints Cosmas and Damian* (1438–1443) would make a striking album cover design, or a poster for the tour (the actual poster for this show is an appropriated *New Yorker* magazine cover). That the saints are not only losing their heads but their eyes too—being blindfolded—provokes a strange awareness of the fact of viewing in the viewer of this decapitating spectacle. Also, that these heads are rolling within the calm, rational perspective of a sunny, Tuscan landscape.

Circles are for the idea of recycling that is itself recycled in the work of Walker. Blood is for the liquid puddles and smears of Smith's *palette paintings*, which are also at least semi-blind in their making. Money is for everything real and abstract that circulates in the practice of Price, whose very name rhymes with money. Blindness is for the technical malfunctions that both produce and disturb the images of Guyton. Price, too, has sometimes caused blindness by entombing visual information in sculptural works, disappearing highly circulated imagery such as terrorist hostage beheadings before the very eyes of his viewers. There is something definitely and strangely headless about Smith's palettes, but his total project can be discussed in terms of recycling as well: his exhibition posters may return in other works for other exhibitions, becoming new paintings, collages, or books, for example. In a way, Walker blinds his digital scanner by smearing its flat eye with toothpaste or chocolate. There is also something bloody in these splotches of mass-produced goodness. Not to mention the recycling of signature Guyton and Walker gestures in the collaborative Guyton/Walker, not represented here.

We could say that the contemporary artist is somehow split between the decapitated saint and the fascinated onlooker or king, and that his work is like the solitary, circular motion of the sword within the frame or conditions of his own production. And here where rolling heads turn to gold, we are also sometimes tempted to imagine another (evil?) recycling that produces nothing of any use and conserves no value. A bachelor machine grinding away for nothing, grinding itself. Because if there are the rational and natural cycles that produce and renew value—the seasons, the fashions, the compost heap, etc.—there are also devious cycles like the ones Jacques Lacan graphed out, that turn on lack and whose very turning erodes and splits identity, producing only missed encounters with the real and endless substitutions.[2] Breasts, for example, that are not really breasts but Polystyrene voids. Or material ejaculations saved and copied as jpeg files. Images that take repetition as their starting point, and do not stop. In the heart of our value-producing circulations, we plug in these machines that transform nothing, that do not progress, and only recycle their own revolutions. Like Duchamp's *Rotoreliefs*, they throb and pulsate in the bustle of the marketplace, infecting the visual and the rational with a corrosive, deviant movement that moves only itself. They work and they do not work. Or maybe it is that they work by decapitating themselves.

A jammed inkjet printer printing out its own dysfunction. A still-wet painter's palette shifted from the table to the wall and presented as a finished work, and that keeps pulling us back down to the idea of a table again. A press release that appears on the desks of different galleries at once and that articulates nothing except that it is assuming the place and function of a press release. A desktop scanner automatically capturing a formless stain or a brick wall. Packaging that contains nothing but itself, or information that becomes its own wrapper, concealing itself in itself. Toothpaste without a tube. Or serially produced canvases, each as energetic and expressive as the next, overstocking four or five gallery booths at the same art fair and sometimes even plastered with posters advertising previous exhibitions at other galleries. An artwork on the glossy cover of *Artforum* re-photographed and re-presented once more, installed there where we want to see the work-work. Stacks and piles of these. Works working on themselves, or else devising ways of standing in for and substituting themselves. Productions of productions, strange duplications, repetitions and reformattings. Commodities that announce their own way of being something other than what they seem, examples of art, etc.

The contemporary artist does not just produce and present objects or images, he produces production itself, presentation itself … images and ideas of these that are at the same time (like it or not) ethical propositions. Like any worker today, the artist's job is also to talk and move, putting words, images and his own body into circulation. More than anything he makes momentum. But there is really no time to think about this now. There is only the possibility of putting this no-time to work and of capturing it in frozen glimpses that are themselves built on speed and work. And any work that holds our attention today is one that not only shows itself, but that it could be otherwise, shows that the relation between an artist and his own activity can always be modified, even interrupted. Art becomes a way of working on the displacement of information from one format to another, and of working on the way we are displaced too, in work and in play. At what point do the boundaries of the artwork dissolve in the momentum that carries it along, and how can this be made visible? And all this—what Jacques Rancière has been calling "the distribution of the sensible"—is precisely a question of politics.

It has been a long while since the time an artist put into his work counted as a valid measure of the work's value. Duchamp and Warhol, with the readymade and serial production, freed art from the old calculus of time and value. Meanwhile, in the so-called real world, the time of production continues to dilate and expand in relation to the shrinking time of paid work, colonizing the unpaid time of speaking, thinking, and consuming too. And back in the art world, there is the growing suspicion that objects are not the only readymades, that the artist himself is the subjective equivalent of a urinal or Brillo box, even. Viewers may notice the glitches and dysfunctions in these exemplary productions signed Guyton, Price, Walker, and Smith and wonder whether they count more as expressive gestures, as accidents, or as moments where design realizes the possibility of escaping itself. Because readymades can also be un-made.

It has been said that under the conditions of contemporary capitalism our work is no longer able to transform anything.[3] It has also been proposed that the artist's gesture no longer has any direct influence over the apparatus that circulates and assigns value to his work.[4] So we are now asking ourselves about the perverse im-potentialities of processes that know how to quit in the middle of their own cycling, that suddenly do nothing with their doing-nothing. The images that hold our attention today are half-lodged and half-disappeared in what circulates them, in the very mechanism they want to picture. They are presentations of this. And within their own rhythms they sometimes seem to open up unexpected spaces of non-work, without even stopping.

Guyton has taken the chrome frames of office chairs, turned them on their sides, and presented them as sculptures. For his last exhibition in New York [at Friedrich Petzel Gallery, 2006], he recycled the poster for the gallery's previous show, superimposing two separate events and the two artistic identities they promoted onto a single document. Such strategies, in addition to the digital reproductions and mechanical accidents in his serially produced canvases, open up the possibility that an artist's gesture is never identical to itself and that its most subversive potential lies in its capacity to make itself slip and stutter in the very moment of its appearance. We could call this inspired, but that would be banal. The work signed Guyton is interesting precisely in the way that it hijacks something like inspiration, interrupting and splitting it from itself, automatically and repeatedly. This is also a kind of politics. Because it is when the materials and the processes themselves are allowed to fold back and infect this thing or moment we always want to call the artistic subject that they meet the possibility of their own emancipation. And we too discover new potentials when our relation to our own products becomes reversible, or when the decisions we make are able to turn around and decide us too.

Price recently produced a "work" consisting of a title (*Grey Flags*, 2006) and a few paragraphs of rambling prose. These were then inserted into different contexts, functioning as the title and press release copy for two exhibitions in two separate New York venues. By reappropriating the tools that mediate and explain our work in both commercial and institutional contexts, we address the fact that our only available means of production today are also and at the same time our common means of communication. For Price, bootlegging and piracy are not merely acts of theft (of content), they are creative transportations and rhythmic interventions. Because if work today can be defined as the movement of information from here to there, the contemporary artist no longer pretends to invent a new language, but instead confronts us with the potential we all share to disrupt both the directionality and the tempo of readymade codes, thereby undermining how these reproduce property relations, for example. The knots, folds, and loops in Price's recent vacuum forms and mylar "films," as well as his use of commercial packaging processes, are sculptural ways of interrogating the artist's capacity to reroute cultural capital. While his silk-screened sheets of clear plastic cause transparency to work against itself when folded or rolled, the opaque Polystyrene panels call our attention to the fact that today the packaging *is* the content, and that it is only by intervening at the moment where format becomes message ("dispersion") that we might regain something like communicability.

Smith is a virtuoso of the shortcut, and although he never seems to quit and is constantly stoking the engines of his own machine, few contemporary artists are so Chaplinesque in their handling of materials and of their own productive rhythms. He recently produced 90 paintings in one week in order to fill an abandoned power station in Memphis, and tomorrow he will plug in his photocopiers and line an entire bookcase with hand-bound volumes of his own drawings. But it would be misleading to celebrate speed and quantity for their own sakes. Smith has volatilized and dispersed the notion of the artistic gesture. There is always his hand, as there was always Picasso's, but in Smith's case the hand has joined forces with any and every available means of mechanical reproduction (no matter how rudimentary and everyday) in order to extend and multiply itself in time and in space. The gesture is there, but it is also there and there, and never exactly equal to itself. The name "Josh Smith," both signature and recurring subject of so many canvases, reminds us that the mark he makes is always already displaced along the constantly bifurcating assembly line of his production. The artistic subject is not identical

to this mark, it is multiplied by it every time, and at the end
of the day will stock a room, stockpiled and stacked and
pushing itself to the point of exhaustion that never seems
to arrive. It is as if he first needs to overwhelm himself with
work before he can start discovering the escape routes
and counter rhythms that are his art. Smith's "style" could
be described as an impossible attempt to reinvent the folk
artist's hand with all the invisible and automatic speeds
that outmode it today.

Walker has a particular way of confronting the
historical legacy of Pop serial production with contemporary technologies of digital reproduction. Not long ago,
he kidnapped the desktop scanner from its normal and
designed purpose, putting it to work as a kitchen cutting
board, a painter's palette, and a camera instead. This could
be described as extreme pro-sumption, or as a delinquent
attempt to cash in on the false promises of user-friendly
technology. Taking this so-called friendship at its word,
Walker then tests its limits, sometimes abusively. His recent
exhibition of enlarged reproductions of Michael Jackson's
identification card, along with images from a television
commercial starring Andy Warhol and his signature recycling
symbols, points to the perverse possibilities lying dormant
within the means by which our culture endlessly repeats
itself, and us along with it. How can copy and paste be
converted into experimental strategies of dis-identification
for the consumer and duplicator of digital media? At what
point does the artist disown his own products, and when
does he decide to let technology take over his gestures?
In Walker's practice, a scanner is not just an available means
of copying images and altering scales; it is itself a potential
site of creative dysfunction, containing within its own
mechanism repressed possibilities of subjective play.
Which is to say that a machine can be made to lose its head,
too, suddenly revealing new and *improper* spaces of projection
where before we only perceived work, repetition, and
efficiency.

Of course a production process can also decide
to behave properly and fill a gallery with objects for passive
enjoyment, striking poses, showing up on time before
moving on again, steadily gaining value, etc. But in New York,
it is always a question of how to put tension into these

performances, how to open things up again, there in the commercial gallery where it seems least likely that any real difference can be produced. The works on view here have mobility built into them from the start, they are, to varying degrees and in different ways, opportunistic; and of course Zurich offers one more opportunity to mobilize some fresh currencies. They knowingly take their chances and make their moves within the conditions they reflect and mediate. There is the Guyton machine, the Price machine, etc., each attempting to elaborate its singularity, its own strange rhythm on this common plane. Their best moments are when they manage to do something concrete and unexpected with this law of equivalence that seeks to conform everything to its own flattening abstraction. And since breaking this law is not as simple as it once seemed, the more effective strategies will from now on involve using flatness, abstraction, and reproduction against themselves, and converting these into forces of heterogeneity instead. Capital never stops its decapitating, so our productions will have to become headless too.

In the poster, armed soldiers are also present, standing by as heads roll and turn to gold, as if guarding the perimeter of a crime scene. Maybe they are museum guards, maybe they are part of the production itself. We also notice hundreds of finely brushed flowers, and the bright, un-splattered stockings of the onlookers in the foreground. In the background, the vertical ramparts of a castle reflect the sunlight. And beyond these, receding green hills crowned with smaller, more distant ramparts. If we have discarded the perspective that once allowed the depiction of such a scenario, we have also multiplied our means of decapitalizing.

[1]   Michael Taussig, *The Magic of the State*, Routledge, London 1997.

[2]   Rosalind Krauss, *The Optical Unconscious*, MIT Press, Cambridge, Massachusetts 1993.

[3]   Paolo Virno, *A Grammar of the Multitude. For an Analysis of Contemporary Forms of Life*, Semiotext(e), New York and Los Angeles 2004.

[4]   Claire Fontaine, "Artistes ready-made et grève humaine: quelques précisions," *Pacemaker*, 9–10 (December 2005), p. 9–10.

The American Action Printer
Vincent Pécoil

Originally published in *Wade Guyton*, exh. cat., La Salle de Bains, Lyon, Les presses du réel, Dijon 2007, p. 73–83.

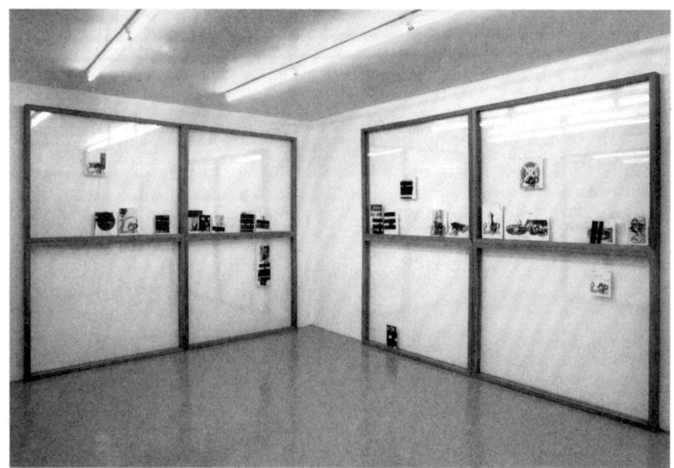

Wade Guyton's art is an art of the double bind: whether he uses printed matter or three-dimensional material, the arrangements of forms and meanings he sets to work seem contradictory. His work unfolds along various antinomies, such as functionalism and decoration, art and industry, original and reproduction. What he calls his *Untitled Action Sculptures* (1998–present), for instance, are based on a series of contradictions between on the one hand, the handmade nature and formless aspect of the pieces, and on the other hand, the rationalist connotation and industrial quality of the original material (in this case, the steel tubular armature of Marcel Breuer chairs, an origin that seems entirely antithetical to the sculpture that results from it). Guyton's objects have been described as "drawings in space," and these *Action Sculptures* are indeed lines that have been transposed into three dimensions, into real space, canceling the drawing/volume dichotomy in the same way the drip in Pollock's paintings brought together color and line, outline and colored plane. At La Salle de Bains, the black sculpture placed in the courtyard acted as a "drawing" of this kind. The piece was like the three-dimensional expression of one of the motifs Guyton has been reusing in various ways, the shape printed on the image of a sculpture that appears on one of the drawings of *Untitled No.1*. Guyton's previous *Action Sculptures* not only relate to one of the most remarkable formal innovations of Action Painting, they also suspend another type of opposition previously considered irreconcilable: that between functional rationalism and expressivity. Guyton's dismantling of the chair, because of its abrupt literalness, suggests that what is at stake is not an allegorical "deconstruction" of its meaning but rather, as in his other works, a kind of double bind, a suspension of its signification. Implicitly, the sculpture is based on an odd coupling: Pollock meets Breuer. Similarly, some images included in what he calls his "printer drawings" place side by side all kinds of random objects: classic modernist sculptures, Constructivist-like drawings, images of dishware or of ornaments, artworks inspired by Surrealism or biomorphic abstraction, as well as an installation view of the *Minimal Art* exhibition at the Gemeentemuseum (The Hague, 1968), over which quadrilateral shapes, bands, or alternating stripes in black or red ink have been printed.

These "printer drawings" are, in fact, pages from art books—exhibition catalogues, monographs, art fair catalogues—or from architecture books. These publications go through the same treatment as old books with rare etchings in the hands of unscrupulous antique dealers: their illustrations are torn out. Then, with a standard inkjet printer, Guyton adds geometrical shapes to the original plates. These printed overlays do not relate to the illustration in any ostensible way. One drawing, for instance, shows a Suprematist composition superimposed over an abstract biomorphic sculpture. Another shows a perforated rectangle over a Dada poster; in another case, flames crawl over reproductions of paintings, like a montage of Photoshop design elements. Selections of these drawings are then inserted in wood frames with double-sided Plexiglas. At La Salle de Bains, there were three sets of four frames.

Thus displayed, the drawings seemed like precious documents that require preservation. At the same time, the way they were distributed in each frame seemed random or disordered, as though some of the drawings had slipped and fallen to the bottom of the frame. By showing the anticipated decay of images preserved like priceless relics, Guyton integrates in its very conception the obsolescence of the work to come.

One effect of these works is to reorient the viewer's attention from the work itself to a new place, or site, which has long ago become the ultimate destination of art: the book (in a generic sense). Indeed, what unfolds in the exhibition space could be called something like *New Design for Showing Books* or *New Design for Showing Images*. In 2003, Guyton created a piece called *New Design*. The sculpture was based on the armature of Dan Graham's *New Design for Showing Videos* (1995). Yet what Guyton's sculpture was really showing was just the armature, just a wooden structure without glass: something to look at instead of a tool for seeing. One of Minimal art's ambitions was to reorient the viewer's attention from the work itself to the physical environment of the gallery. Conceptual art extended this reorientation to the general context of the reception of the work, by attempting, as was the case with Graham's piece, to raise the consciousness of viewers about their place and their role as spectators. At the same time as they were viewing art (videos) through the glass panels, the viewers inside Graham's *New Design for Showing Videos* saw their own reflection, as well as the reflection of other potential viewers, blending in with the image on the monitor. Large enough to encompass the entire reflected silhouette of a viewer, the frames of Guyton's *Untitled No.1*, *No.2*, and *No.3* extend Graham's dialectic a step further. Like formal reminiscences of *New Design* (2003), the sets of frames act like structures for the display of printed images, except they are placed against the wall rather than in space, as though Graham's piece had been flattened. Beyond their immediate physical environment, they incorporate a larger cultural context: that other site of art that is the world of the reproduced image.

Among the source images on which geometric shapes are printed are a number of images of abstract works: Op art, biomorphic abstraction, Action painting, hard-edge abstraction, and more. Guyton does not exploit these images in a cynical way, like a repertoire of equivalent signs. On the contrary, by bringing to the same level these various reproductions of abstract or quasi-abstract works, like Marcel Duchamp's *Passage from Virgin to Bride*, he rather points toward the tendency of art history books to transform abstraction into imagery. Guyton is not exclusively interested in abstraction. The recurrent combination of images of sculptures, paintings, and design furniture points to the forced integration of disparate art forms that occurs in the devices of art history, i.e., the book and the museum.

As in Duchamp's *Large Glass*, the placement of drawings at different levels within a frame creates a distinction between several "dimensions." In the same way that the black sculpture in the courtyard could be considered as the three-dimensional reality of the related drawing from *Untitled No.1*, the drawings placed closest to the top in all three sets of frames suggest an additional dimension of art, a separate realm like the Bride's Domain in the *Large Glass*. That domain, like a hypothetical dimension—the fourth or the nth—might be the realm of history, the other space of art, its imaginary site. *Untitled No.2* brought together a Stella painting covered with flames, a famous Alexander Liberman canvas shown in the *Responsive Eye* exhibition at MoMA and customized here with red and black stripes, some sort of biomorphic abstraction drawing with similar superimposed elements, and a painting by Duchamp. In another frame, one could glimpse Duchamp's *Rotoreliefs* stuck between a few abstract modernist sculptures, some baroque-looking drinking glasses, and a Constructivist drawing. In *Untitled No.3*, vintage modern art is juxtaposed with ancient ornamental objects; some pages come from art fair catalogues, underscoring the other final destination of these objects, their circulation as commodities for trade—a finality that was also suggested in the triangular Stella in *Untitled No.1*, titled *Leo Castelli*.

The grouping of frames from *Untitled No.1* reinforce the analogy between art and design by presenting works of art, for example a painting by Albers covered with stripes, next to images from the decorative arts, like a printed fabric with abstract patterns. The recurring trope of alternate green and red stripes not only acquires in Guyton's work the function of a "mark" or of a personal style, it also cannot help but recall other famous striped paintings, like Stella's or Buren's. Here, however, the trope returns to its printed origin: the striped printed endpaper. The stripes—in the same way as the grids—act as devices blocking out and obliterating the subject, and decorating it too. This juxtaposition of images and abstract patterns recalls the way abstraction, coordinated with other figures, has moved into the realm of graphic design, an evolution Guyton hinted at in the tide of his show at the Kunstverein in Hamburg and at Friedrich Petzel Gallery, *Color, Power & Style*, an allusion to the title of New Order's 1983 album *Power, Corruption & Lies*, whose cover, designed by Peter Saville, consists of geometric shapes superimposed over a Fantin-Latour painting. This back and forth movement between figures, decorative abstract patterns, and abstract painting is nothing new: the image reproduced on the announcement card of the Salle de bains show is a detail of one of the "printer drawings" featuring a painting by Frank Stella titled *Sinjerli II* (1967), from a series of works themselves inspired by ornamental patterns of a purely decorative nature, whose reproduction was excerpted from the monograph on Stella written by Wiliam Rubin and published by MoMA.

What is specific to Guyton, however, is his situation as an artist in relationship to this issue. In his essay on Stella, Rubin noted that, "Stella is one of the first major painters in the modern tradition to have been formed virtually entirely through the practice of abstract art."[1] A comparable statement could be made for Guyton in terms of Appropriation art: he is one of the first and most important artists of his generation to have been formed through the postmodern practice of appropriation, and for whom abstraction has always existed, above all, as a reproduced image. Guyton's decision to use printed images as his raw material is somewhat natural. But at the same time, this familiarity with the appropriation process is the source of a certain malaise and a kind of recoiling from the practice itself. Appropriation has become common practice. It has itself been appropriated, not only because so many artists continue to use it, but also because the process has been co-opted by other fields: it has become, for instance, an advertising gimmick. Instead of a complacent yielding to this widespread usage of recycling, Guyton's leveling of images appears like a source of anxiety.[2]

By presenting this kind of flattening and standardization of art through its images, by these incongruous juxtapositions and superimposed layers, Guyton's art functions like an anamnesis of the avant-garde's wayward fate (now that it has become an instrument of the cultural industry) and the more general destiny of all works of the modern era: to end up as a photograph. This art can be understood as an apocryphal form of institutional critique whose target would be Malraux's "imaginary museum." As the latter once wrote: "For the last hundred years, art history [...] has been the history of that which can be photographed."[3] Guyton's torn-out art-book pages, with their overlaid Photoshop-made patterns, are like a demonstration *ad absurdum* of this declaration. Malraux used to say of black-and-white photography that it brought the photographed objects closer together, draining them of their different colors, materials, and dimensions in favor of a common style. Guyton stages the effects of this leveling, accentuating it further by his layering of patterns and images. The imaginary museum's universal library is an unreal but coherent world, an extension of the world of real, tangible art. The "museum without walls" imposes order with schools, styles, and periods. The disorder within Guyton's frames evokes the frailty of that construction, the weakness of its coherence. Using the same method as in his "printer drawings," Guyton also creates prints on canvas, which he calls *paintings*. Like the drawings, the canvases are filled with images and patterns utilizing an inkjet printer. Guyton provokes a number of "accidents" during printing, by yanking the fabric down or to the side, letting "events" disturb the tranquility of the photographic image. In so doing, he inaugurates a new era, that of "action printing," a two-dimensional correlate of his *Action Sculptures*. But the action printer's "existential arena" is no longer the canvas, as Harold Rosenberg described it,[4] but rather the arena without walls of the imaginary museum, the sum of all reproducible images.

The deliberately homemade, imperfect, or even "failed" aspect of the printed drawings and paintings is a singular way of reacting, at an individual level, to a historical situation locked in a permanent one-upmanship of sophistication and an inflation of production; a time when important events (biennials, blockbuster exhibitions, etc.) drag art into a hopeless competition with the powers of entertainment. But the use of inkjet printers is also a symbol of the evolution of the modes of production and the collective organization of labor in contemporary societies. At the beginning of the 20th century, the Russian art historian and critic Nikolai Tarabukin imagined the move of art and image-making technology from the easel to the machine, from handmade confection to industrial production. In fact, the cultural industry fulfilled this program in the 20th century, a historical irony that resurfaced in Warhol's Factory when he symbolically diverted the principles of the modern division of labor to his studio and appropriated its formats (film, television, mechanical production …). The evolution proposed by Guyton is no less significant. By using office technology, he integrates at a symbolic level in his work the passage of contemporary economies from industrial production to the service sector. Shifting from the factory to the office, the studio becomes the site where images are organized, digitized, and circulated, rather than a site of production.

By reproducing digital images of the "printer drawings" at almost their original scale, by pretending to replace them in their original context, the present catalogue underscores, if perversely, the affirmation of the book as a space or site of art. The move of these fragments from the museum without walls into the office-studio is not without risk: like the flames threatening Ed Ruscha's *Los Angeles County Museum of Art on Fire*, the images are devoured by flames like another decorative element. Thus supplemented with hot-rod imagery, the works by Stella and Ronald Davis are placed next to a press photograph showing a race riot, thus pointing toward multiple chains of references: to the event itself, to the press' covering of it, to Warhol, and to Guyton's artist peer and friend Kelley Walker. Guyton's imaginary museum in flames is no serene oasis, and the images he exhibits are anxious images, whose status is uncertain, and whose form and placement are more accidental than essential.

As in the drawings, the black and red areas shaped like dots, bands, or quadrilaterals sometimes cover the

entire image, forming several abstract layers. This affinity
for the palimpsest might appear to be a concession to
the notion of a general equivalence of historical forms. But
this is not the case: rather, it is Guyton's personal way of
confronting the specific cultural situation in which abstraction has turned into imagery—its transformation into
printed matter. Today, abstract art is always *already* an image.
Any line, dot, or shape is now susceptible to a recalling of a
preexisting abstract work. Guyton is simply using a shortcut:
images of sculptures and paintings become the basis of the
work. Yet he does not subscribe to the complacent hypoth-
esis of a post-historical moment. His superimpositions are
not a gratuitous form of mélange. He does not presuppose,
like some of his contemporaries who seek to justify their
own practice, that we have entered a post-historical era in
which the modernist period has come to an end and artists
are liberated from history, free to pick any styles in the
historical trash heap and cobble them together ... Guyton,
who is familiar with the "strategic" approach developed
by Yve-Alain Bois (and before him by Hubert Damisch), does
not share this perspective of a generalized equivalence of
historical forms.[5] In fact, his "printer drawings" and their
placement suggest a significantly different model of the
unfolding of history than that proposed by modernist histo-
riography. Rather than the latest revolutionary development,
his work can be considered within the framework of a cumulative historical process, an accretion of various movements
instead of a succession of revolutions. One could describe
it as a cumulative accretion of Pop (a form of realism whose
subjects are the products of the cultural industry), Minimal
art (with its own Pop borrowings), Conceptual art (a radical
synthesis of the previous two), and 1980s Appropriation art,
which was itself a convergence of these different practices.

The current economic and cultural environment
reifies any intellectual innovation as a style or a brand.
In this context of the generalized branding of contemporary
life,[6] the appropriation of preexisting forms has a newfound
critical legitimacy. The process of appropriation is not
used to force the historical status of a work through a self-
justifying quotation ("See how educated I am and how
seamlessly I inscribe myself in history and tradition").
Rather, it integrates within artistic practice the state of

art in a world where the cultural industry has brought to completion (though in a distorted way) the old avant-garde project of dissolving art in the totalizing sphere of environment-as-art. The "strategy" (in Yve-Alain Bois' sense) employed by Guyton consists in reaching a kind of stalemate in the sense that his work can no longer be formally co-opted. The game in question is played with several adversaries at once, including the cultural industry, art history and the artist's own peers. Like many other artists today, Guyton practices a non-reversible form of appropriation, an appropriation that can no longer be appropriated by the realms of advertising, graphic design, or interior architecture—until new application.

[1] William Rubin, *Frank Stella*, The Museum of Modern Art, New York 1970, p. 8.

[2] See, in this regard, Johanna Burton's very interesting statement in *Texte zur Kunst*, June 2006, p. 186: "I feel he actually poses the question about this kind of comfort we have today with constantly circulating signs. Less than feeling comfortable, I feel like this work often professes a real anxiety, and doesn't feel that it actually belongs in the history it invokes at all. There is a kind of disconnection that happens, actually. And in creating disconnections, he allows the particularity of certain kinds of appropriate signs to actually become general [...] You think you know what these signs are, but in fact they are often rendered very mute and very citational, as opposed to referential. They are very much less transparent than works by so many other artists who are just referring to things that seem very obvious and clearly legible. There is an illegibility to some of his work that I find very interesting. A kind of stubbornness that I don't think has to do with his feeling comfortable, so much as with feeling unsure about his own procedures."

[3] André Malraux, *Le Musée imaginaire*, Gallimard, Paris 1965, p. iii.

[4] Harold Rosenberg, "The American Action Painters," in *The Tradition of the New*, Horizon Press, New York 1960.

[5] The text Guyton decided to reproduce in *New York Twice*, the catalogue of the exhibition curated by Fabrice Stroun in 2005 for Air de Paris, was "Painting: The Task of Mourning," by Yve-Alain Bois; *Endgame: Reference and Simulation in Recent Painting and Sculpture*, MIT Press, Cambridge, Massachusetts 1986.

[6] See, on this issue, the discussion between Guyton and Kelley Walker in *Guyton/Walker. The Failever of Judgement*, JRP|Ringier, Zurich 2005, p. 45, 47, and 53.

Review: Wade Guyton, Friedrich Petzel Gallery
Holland Cotter

Originally published in *The New York Times*, "Art in Review" column, December 14, 2007, p. E38.

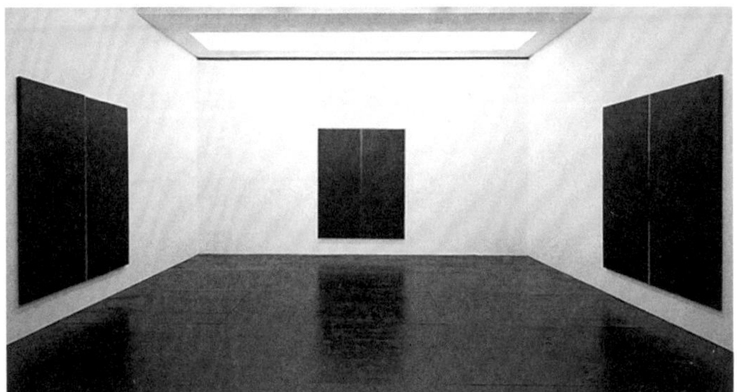

View of the exhibition *Wade Guyton*, Friedrich Petzel Gallery, New York, 2007

Wade Guyton's show of new paintings looks at first like a garage-band version of Mark Rothko's somber Houston chapel, made even darker by sheets of black-painted plywood covering the gallery floor. As is his custom, Mr. Guyton takes modernism, with its touchy-feely spiritual pretensions, for a hard ride. And as always he goes well beyond a one-line put-down. The art-into-life aesthetic of John Cage and the painting-into-architecture aesthetic of Blinky Palermo would seem to be among his models.

All the paintings in the show are large and abstract. Made up of faint patterns of horizontal and vertical lines on a black ground, they suggest early Frank Stella pinstripes in progress, or inkedover Agnes Martins. The medium really is ink, though not applied by hand. Each painting is made up of edge-to-edge black rectangles applied to linen by an Epson inkjet printer. A central vertical line in each work marks where the linen was folded to fit the printer's width. Other lines result from accidents of printing and reprinting the incrementally placed rectangles that make up each piece.

Accident is Mr Guyton's modus operandi. He hit on the monochromatic format while making other kinds of paintings, traces of which remain under some of the present works. Yet he never entirely relinquishes control: periodic tugs at the linen during printing affected the patterns and tones.

The creaky plywood floor he has laid down—a replica of the one in his studio—reinforces a sense of impurity and instability, un-modernist if not necessarily anti-modernist, like late Ad Reinhardt. It also contributes to making the show, so laconic and adamant, a knockout total experience, one of the memorable gallery sights of the season.

Rites of Silence
Johanna Burton

Originally published in *Artforum*, XLVI, no. 10, Summer 2008, p. 364–373.

Untitled, 2007
Epson UltraChrome inkjet on linen, 213.4 × 175.3 cm

Just who does he think he is?
Poised in front of Wade Guyton's
work, admirers and detractors alike
often find themselves asking the
same question. It is not so much
a query regarding the artist's
character—though of course it is
partially that, too—but rather the
expression of a genuine quandary,
one that can feel so basic that it
is hard to find the way to frame it.
Where is he coming from? is another
way to put it, and it may be a little
closer to the mark. But the real
question is rather, and perhaps
simply: How are we to understand
Guyton's relationship to what he
makes? And following from that:
Why do the oblique contours of
this relationship seem to announce
themselves as the very content of
the work?

Consider two of Guyton's one-
person shows mounted in the past
six months, the first at Friedrich
Petzel Gallery in New York, the second at Galerie Chantal Crousel in
Paris. While a group of unique works

was produced for each, Guyton would seem at first glance to have presented nearly carbon-copy exhibitions. In both instances, the artist laid down a false floor made of plywood sheets painted a dense black, the kind of black that seems at once to reflect and suck up light. On the walls were hung large-scale paintings, described in the respective—also nearly identical—press releases as "ostensibly black monochromes." *Ostensible* is a fantastic word, and it goes some way in addressing Guyton's work. Etymologically, it derives from the Latin *ostensus*, "to show," but this connotation of transparency is joined by one of skepticism. There is something being shown, but there is also something that is *not* being shown, that is being blocked from view. Synonymous with *allegedly*, *ostensibly* also implies that a claim has been made, that a statement has been drafted, but that there is simply no verifiable proof to back it. That which is ostensible looks like, sounds like, even feels like what it purports to be, but it flashes doubt like a striptease, asking that we believe *and* interrogate simultaneously.

Such operations, though seemingly discovered afresh every decade, have long been the purview of certain practices of painting. Indeed, the past 40 years of critical discourse have taken as foundational the idea that it is perhaps *only* its ostensible nature that keeps contemporary painting from relinquishing all relevance. This does not mean that a deeply held, intuitively argued belief in painting qua painting is not still in effect. (These days, a phrase like "the function of painting" has a 50-50 chance of being met with an eye roll— one more eerie similarity between this era and the 1980s.) What it means, rather, is simply that those who cannot quite accept the notion of painting's radical authenticity have long looked for its first principles outside the frame. Take, for instance, the following passage, which would seem to address Guyton's ostensible monochromes astutely enough:

> It is fundamental to X's work that it function in complicity with those very institutions it seeks to make visible as the necessary condition of the artwork's intelligibility. This is the reason that his work not only appears in museums and galleries, but also poses as painting. It is only thereby possible for his work to ask: What makes it possible to see a

painting? What makes it possible to see a painting *as a painting?* And, under such conditions of its presentation, to what end painting?

My telltale substitution of the generic placeholder "X" for a proper name is likely clue enough that this is borrowed text and that it does not describe Guyton's paintings at all. As it happens, these are Douglas Crimp's words, from his 1981 essay "The End of Painting," with the subject of his analysis being, perhaps unsurprisingly, Daniel Buren.[1] Who better to exemplify the contextual turn born of the 1960s and 1970s—a shift that allowed for the very conditions of artistic production and reception to become content? And how useful might it prove to think through the implications of one of the original purveyors of institutional critique for an artist, in this case Guyton, whose practice would seem, if not exactly aligned with, nonetheless clearly indebted to the older figure? Buren had his factory-produced textile stripes, Guyton has his equally terse black squares spit out of an ink-jet printer; surely this is a neat transposition of strategies from an industrial to a postindustrial context. In the end, though, while the comparison is indeed quite useful, what turns out to be most illuminating are the differences, not the correspondences, that it reveals.

For however uncannily germane to Guyton's practice Crimp's language might initially seem, the critic's analysis ultimately proves wholly inapplicable to the younger artist's work, and the very disjunction in fact sheds some light on greater shifts in the terms of art making over the past 40 years. If in 1981, Buren continued to hold out promise for critical practice, it was precisely because his work did *not* read legibly within the language of painting it alluded to. As Crimp put it in his essay's closing gambit, while Buren's work was of course literally visible, it was at odds with any historicist account of painting, and therefore did not register within painting's terms. Crimp's projection for the future was clear: "At the moment when Buren's work becomes visible, the code of painting will have been abolished and Buren's repetitions can stop: the end of painting will have been finally acknowledged." Buren was just as confident about the deep ramifications of his own ideas. Quoted in Crimp's essay is a passage from the artist's 1977 volume

Reboundings, wherein Buren claims the highest stakes for his work: "It is no longer a matter even of challenging the artistic system. Neither is it a matter of taking delight in one's interminable analysis. The ambition of this work is quite different. It aims at nothing less than abolishing the code that has until now made art what it is, in its production and in its institutions."[2] Whether Buren succeeded or failed in these aspirations and whether his subsequent anointment by the very "art history" against which he chafed signals an abolishment or an expansion of said code are questions for another time (and I am certainly not the first to raise them). But the fact that Buren is today so much acknowledged by art-historical discourse—such that the tenets of institutional critique are now readily accepted by institutions themselves—presents a conundrum of sorts for any artist who would seek to make "critical" art. Pointing to the context for painting, or for art making more generally, as Guyton does, is inevitably attended by the peril of merely mimicking gestures of the past that, in this changed historical situation, are reduced to motif. We therefore need to ask how artists might best extrapolate from the discursive tussles of Buren's time, pondering how and to what end an artist such as Guyton might be keeping the "end of painting" at bay or, perhaps more aptly, keeping the death of painting alive.

Looking closely at the works in question, one notes that if Guyton is himself working toward the dismantling of codes (or, perhaps more realistically, the rerouting of them), he is not founding his project on the nullification of painting or on its transformation into an illegible cipher: if his are "ostensibly" black monochromes, in other words, it is not due to any confusion whatsoever about the status of these objects as paintings. That is to say that what is "ostensible" here really *is* the denomination "black monochrome," and not painting itself. Though obviously following a format, Guyton's monochromes have none of the built-in regularity of, say, Buren's stubborn 8.7-centimeter-wide alternating cloth stripes (which have in their way taken on uber-aesthetic status despite their original somewhat anti-aesthetic premise). In fact, the opposite is true. Despite being produced by way of a set of predetermined, extremely limited rules, and without a drop of paint or a single brushstroke, they bear all the obvious residues of spontaneous (and therefore "immediate") mark making. Having folded lengths of factory-primed linen so that each half equals the width of his Epson UltraChrome large-format printer (44 inches), Guyton runs them through the machine, which deploys hundreds of individual ink-jet heads. Together, these tiny, dumb mechanical soldiers labor at Guyton's behest to produce just as dumb an "image": a black rectangle, drawn and then "filled" by Guyton in Photoshop, is printed twice, once on each side of his folded linen, doubling, in essence, the image of the rectangle (at the same time as trying to unite its parts on one field). Depending on the effects of the initial printing process, Guyton opts to run one side or the other (or sometimes both) through the machine a second and sometimes third time (or more), smoothing and filling prior snags and drags on the one hand and on the other providing an even denser surface on which new anomalies can occur. To the extent that Guyton's enterprise could be seen as one invested in the technics of image production, it figures technology's tendency to complicate, rather than simplify— that is, to make its own kind of mess. And truth be told, Guyton aids and abets the glitches, gagging his printer with material not meant for it, and asking it to lay uniform sheets of ink over an expanse twice its size—feats hardly enumerated in the user's manual. In fact, if Guyton has a technical skill per se, it might be defined as encouraging malfunctions.

Once the canvas has been fed through the printer, it drops unceremoniously to the floor and accordingly picks up evidence of its time there in scratches, dings, and dust. The resulting two sides of the rectangle—given the imprecise procedure of simply folding the canvas in half and temporarily taping its edges together—are rarely if ever perfectly aligned; rather, one side typically is slightly higher or lower than the other. And one side, or both, may register the marks of having wandered diagonally offtrack during printing before being pulled back into alignment; this sometimes produces a kind of shuttered effect, almost photographic in its unintended illusion of light (the primed canvas) peeking out from between regimented lines that no longer match up to form an uninterrupted solid. The ink, trying to fix itself to a ground that is designed to hold thicker pigment, also occasionally pools, smudges, and drips.

And of course, every piece of linen, once unfolded, bears the mark of the central seam, not so much a "zip" as a kind of vertical navel.[3] Each painting thus bears proof of its process—the one real constant in every iteration of the series. (Or at least, the only readily apparent one: there is also the single digital "source" that is the foundation of all the monochromes—an image file on Guyton's computer with the hard-core-sounding name "bigblack.tif," which, when opened, reveals a comically unassuming little black rectangle.)

The urge to act the connoisseur and genealogize in the face of these works is palpable as, somewhat counter-intuitively, all these procedures result in unadulterated visual pleasure of the kind often associated with abstraction in its more luscious manifestations. Hung sparingly on white walls, the paintings take on the stark elegance we attribute to a whole lineage of morphologically similar items. Names, from Rothko to Reinhardt and Stella to Marden, are apt to fly. But let us not forget that these are ostensible monochromes only. They are, none of them, fully resolved, not *really* monochromes, because the measure of their success rests largely on their gesturing to monochrome-ness without ever really getting there. Indeed, a few of the most beautiful canvases—which register thread-thin lines spread nearly an inch apart from one another—are also the most minimal. They were not, however, produced because the cartridge was running dry, as one might think—the problem is not too little ink but, in a sense, too *much*, as the machine over-loads itself in an attempt to carry out Guyton's bidding over and over again. With nearly all its jet heads clogged by ink that has built up and coagulated, the printer barely sputters out a trace of the image it is asked to compulsively repeat. The delicate, visually complex composition that accrues is nothing more than evidence that the Epson "self-clean" function has not kicked in when it ought to.

So what are we to make of all this? Guyton's process is steeped in embarrassingly elementary moves: preselecting basic parameters such as whether to print "draft" or "econ-omy," at "speed" or "quality" rate, and according to "normal," "fine," or "photo" standards—and then simply pushing "print"—comprises most of the artist's control over the work he produces. (The critic inevitably wonders whether it is, after all, worth spilling this much ink on, well, the vicissitudes of spilled ink.) And yet he pairs this embarrassment with another one: that of making undeniably aesthetic products. (Here Guyton's works would seem to perform themselves as decoys inciting the urge for art-historical roll-calling—a kind of bald "ostensibility" that might appear all too well attuned to the current vogue for generic "appropriative" gestures.) Taken together, however, these qualities imply an awareness that a work of art's motioning toward another that came before it does not necessarily bear out much meaning; and an assumption that the binary poles of pining homage and violent erasure are the only two ways to read such allusions is just another mode of marketing. Guyton's recent series of black paintings nods, if mutely, toward this crossroads, in which engagements with discursive history and profiteering usurpations of it look more and more similar. For if today it is impossible not to recognize the lessons handed down by Buren and others, it is likewise impossible not to see how those lessons themselves have been incorporated as a kind of affirmative content. If the language of "abolishing the code" has itself *become* code, what can one say in retort or even in response?[4]

> Finally, a personal incident, which will nicely introduce the figures to come: Thursday, March 9, fine afternoon, I go out to buy some paints (Sennelier inks) –> bottles of pigment: following my taste for the names (golden yellow, sky blue, brilliant green, purple, sun yellow, rose carthame—a rather intense pink), I buy sixteen bottles. In putting them away, I knock one over: in sponging up, I make a new mess: little domestic complications ... And now, I am going to give you the official name of the spilled color, a name printed on the small bottle (as on the others vermilion, turquoise, etc.): it was the color called Neutral (obviously I had opened this bottle first to see what kind of color this Neutral was, about which I am going to be speaking for 13 weeks). Well, I was both punished and disappointed: punished because Neutral spatters and stains (it is a type of dull gray-black); disappointed because Neutral is a color like the others, and for sale (therefore, Neutral is not

> unmarketable): the unclassifiable is classified
> -> all the more reason for us to go back to discourse,
> which, at least, cannot say what the Neutral is.[5]

The spring of 1978 found Roland Barthes doing his own ruminating on the vicissitudes of spilled ink and giving his second lecture series at the Collège de France. Over several months, he introduced and expounded on a term that, nonetheless, he had no intention of ever fully pinning down: "the Neutral."[6] Summing the course up for the school's compulsory annual report, Barthes wrote of his topic that "one studies what one desires or what one fears; within this perspective, the authentic title of the course could have been: *The Desire for Neutral*." He continues, "The argument of the course has been the following: we have defined as pertaining to the Neutral every inflection that, dodging or baffling the paradigmatic, oppositional structure of meaning, aims at the suspension of the conflictual basis of discourse." Presented not as a progressively building argument but instead as an offering of 23 figures or "twinklings," Barthes's exploration of the Neutral includes an argument for silence as one of the incarnations of his fugitive concept. The word —*silence*—should perhaps be treated with some circumspection here; as Barthes points out, he is himself *speaking* about it. Indeed, silence as defined by Barthes, like many of the figures he presents, does not conform to our likely expectations. Silence—like the Neutral itself—is not a passive condition but rather one voluptuously active, so active in fact that it refuses to settle into or onto a singularly readable position. If this sounds dangerously close to a kind of willy-nilly, fleeting lack of commitment, it of course risks being so (but only when it is not *actually* Neutral); for an active silence, as Barthes puts it, is what lies at the heart of all rigorous discourse. It opposes dogmatic speech *and* dogmatic silence alike.

As the foregoing may hint, an obvious tension regarding politics is characteristic of much of Barthes' late work.[7] His suggestion that endlessly articulated battles between opposing opinions might be less potentially subversive than what remains unstated ("the implicit is a crime, because the implicit is a thought that escapes power") is understandably met with frustration by those in circumstances demanding nothing less than out-and-out activism. But Barthes' was, again, not a dictum to be consumed and applied. It was a methodological manifestation of *desire*— full if unfulfilled, and quite analogous to his (disappointed) dream of a truly neutral ink, without color or body; a desire that had all manner of political implications, not the least being that, as one commentator put it, Barthes' writing marked a lifelong project with "no motor other than desire."[8]

Guyton, too, seems, if not programmatically, to put forward a kind of Neutral deportment, one that, per Barthes, "postulates a right to be silent." That does not, of course, keep his commentators from ascribing, almost compulsively (and often aggressively), content and intent. (Indeed, Barthes's worry about silence is that while it begins as a "weapon assumed to outplay the paradigms," it too "congeals itself into a sign.") It's hard to imagine a more overdetermined space than the site of the monochrome—the *black* monochrome no less, that tried-and-true image that now virtually screams out its simultaneous status as tabula rasa and tabula finitum. But if it seems that Guyton, at 36 years old, has reached this point much too early—what avenues has he left open for himself, one wonders while looking at so many iterations of the high-culture sign for "That's all, folks"— it is worth considering the ways in which his career has proceeded by way of such impasses, with such seeming foreclosures levied to hold open future possibilities.

It is not unfair, I hope, to characterize Guyton's oeuvre to date as evincing a certain productive panic when it comes to rendering transparent the reality of being an artist who is faced with the task of making things. He absorbed the lessons of modernism and then postmodernism as an undergraduate in Knoxville, Tennessee, only to arrive in New York in 1996 with a head full of images and ideas that, learned as they were at a slight delay, were no longer quite contemporary. With a certain wariness, Guyton—who for the record, no matter how much attention this essay pays to painting, is not strictly a painter—then set to work entering the dialogue he had previously engaged almost exclusively by way of mediation (art history books, theoretical anthologies, this magazine). He made sculpture: quirky quasi-Minimalist forms in wood or cork that took up too much or too little space; barely held-together strips of

mirrored Plexiglas whose accordion forms reflected viewers
back in tall-skinny sections (a pathetically glittery effect
at once carnivalesque and dance-clubby). By 2001, some of
Guyton's sculptural renderings had taken a turn toward
the disembodied. He found or took photographs—mostly
of architecture, mostly banal—and then altered them using
a black Sharpie to blot out selected features of the images,
producing studies for sculptures that could never be realized,
except possibly through some science-fictional techniques,
since the sculptures he envisioned were essentially holes in
space. Voiding the image but leaving its method of excision
visible, Guyton's *Drawing for Sculpture the Size of a House* (2002)
made the contours of a low-slung American ranch house
into a nameless one-dimensional shape, its jutting angles
now mere geometry. (An unusually dramatic version of this
kind of rendering was produced in *Drawing for Perpetually
Burning Object*, 2002, in which an image of a blocky *something*,
presumably a building, ravaged by angry flames becomes,
with the architecture Sharpied out, a kind of Dantean night-
mare.) For an "actual" sculpture, which he was asked to
make for a public-art show in Brewster, New York, the artist,
after scouring the area to no inspirational avail, landed on
a heap of scrap wood in an alley, more or less neatly abandoned by its previous user when whatever task he or she was
working on was finished. Guyton de- and then reassembled
the pile, arranging it exactly as he had found it, except turned
precisely on its head. (The resulting "sculpture" looked almost
identical to the raw materials.) That Guyton was not really
making a particular kind of material "his own"—or better
said, that his use of the readymade or found object seemed
to result mostly in disappearing objects rather than claiming
or really "transforming" them—seems fundamental to his
practice in retrospect.

But this reaching toward things only to partially and
rather heavy-handedly efface them was after all a *grasping*,
and it offered itself as an insight that could be deployed
procedurally only after Guyton worked more circumspectly
than usual, one day in 2002, to mark a large black "X" over
a page he had ripped from a design magazine. He used a
ruler, and the lines were more or less straight, but not really,
and the unevenness of the ink made the "X" look more
handmade, less dispassionate, than he had wanted it to.

It also took much too long to produce, considering how dumb a gesture it was meant to be. Ripping another page from his stack of magazines and books, he fed it through his home printer (this one little and cheap: an Epson, but no Ultra) after plugging in a ridiculously high point size and typing one giant letter into an otherwise blank Word document: "X."

To say that suddenly Guyton's hands were thus untied would make the change too profound and too definitively liberating. In fact, the rounds of "printer drawings" that ensued and that have continued apace, all of which use book or magazine pages as supports, may let Guyton off the hook for producing their "content"; but in so doing, they render more visible, and thus put more pressure on this choice to let other images speak to some extent on his behalf. However much he laces his found pages with varia printed atop them, they remain partially their own, pulled rudely from their bindings and thus displaced into their new, not wholly transparent contexts. The imagery Guyton generated to superimpose on these backgrounds was limited at first to oversize "X"s but was soon joined by "U"s, colored dots and lines, squares, holes, grids, and other such not-designs constructed with letters or shapes made using Microsoft Word's "drawing tool." Also entering the mix in a few instances were three-dimensional objects, such as a wooden triangle, placed directly on the scanner, and, more often, a handful of "generic" images scanned from other sources and vetted through Photoshop (consistent favorites being "fire" and alternating green and red stripes, both swiped from book jackets). Take, for example, an untitled drawing from 2005, in which Guyton imposes his forcefully cheery green and red stripes over a page from an art book bearing a picture of a pastel Morris Louis painting from 1962. The placement of Guyton's stamp (one that is of course borrowed, not quite his own) on that of Louis (for a Louis is always recognizable as such, and here doubly so, since its caption is visible) neither cancels out the "first" image nor fully articulates a relationship to it. Yet this doubling gesture is still seemingly "readable," in much the same way that a series of "action sculptures" the artist has produced since 2002 is: high-design mid-century furniture is taken apart and manhandled into a lyric but ridiculous new form, but will always remain, and will always be recognizable as, Breuer chairs.

Guyton's decision in 2003 to also begin producing what would eventually become "paintings," first on raw, unstretched linen and soon thereafter on primed and stretched canvas, would seem to be distinctly different from the kind of tête-à-tête pairings of background source image and added superimposition created by the drawings, with their strangely tender yet proprietary urge. But Guyton's stretched paintings of the past few years, no less than the pages torn directly from books, acknowledge what writer Bettina Funcke has called the "risk of images," which she describes as the ethical and conceptual precipice arrived at by artists who participate in image recycling.[9] Some of these paintings appear stridently minimal, "X"s alone or multiplied and advancing in uneven rows, their typeface bodies subtly shifting under the eye (since some were printed directly from digital files and so are crisp and clear, while others are scans of previous works Guyton has produced and have thus experienced "loss"). Others are nearly baroque: multiple, nauseously Pop-colored "U"s are consumed by Guyton's flame; a black square and four random white circles overtly court anthropomorphism, the seemingly gaping holes approximating open-eyed vacuity even while insisting that this is just abstraction after all. What is imported from the world of preexisting imagery becomes confused with what is mapped out within the purview of Photoshop and Word. The "printer drawings'" back- and foregrounds are more clearly distinguished by such overdetermined content as pages occupied first by Broodthaers, Farnsworth, Caro, and Stella, and subsequently by Guyton; the paintings appear to have flattened such distinctions. Yet in producing through their more general nature—their ability to conjure a Rodchenko or a Black Flag logo or anything in between— even *more* references, they seem ever more tethered to citation, if less stably so. A "printer painting" in which the ink-jets have almost sputtered out, leaving us with an ostensible black monochrome that has nearly become an ostensible white monochrome, discloses nothing, and so discloses everything.

"If I were to describe it in a word I should say that I have been like a cartridge that's jammed." So says Henry

Miller, in "The Angel Is My Watermark!" a semiparodic, nearly 20-page episode in *Black Spring* in which the author relates "the genesis of a masterpiece."[10] Living before the Staples epoch, Miller was presumably referring to a firearm, not a balky LaserJet. Yet his mention of a jammed cartridge is serendipitous on several levels. In their too-muchness and not-enoughness, Guyton's works are almost uncannily illuminated via a reading of Miller's characteristically manic reflections on the necessary interplay of erasure and inscription in the (supposedly purely additive) "act of creation." Poking fun at—yet clearly enamored of— myths of genius, Miller enumerates a process of conceiving, in his artist's notepad, a complex layering of drawn and painted images, all of them symbolically ripe but none of them *working*. Having decided, after two excruciating days, that the endeavor has failed, he finally scrubs the wretched thing in the sink and, of course, what does not wash away is the unexpected magnum opus—"It's like a splinter under the nail," he says. Despite the tongue in cheek, Miller— that self-professed jammed cartridge—concedes that there is truth to his parable: "I have never been able to draw a balance. I am always *minus* something. I have a reason therefore to go on."

That there is a certain romanticism to quoting Miller on painting (writing in 1936 as he was, an expat in France, surrounded on all sides by the good and the bad of avant-garde heroics) is unavoidable, but in the end this is perhaps a fair—if also perhaps an unexpected—treatment of Guyton's work. Emphatic discussions of his art have focused on his clear attendance to "modernism," by way of his recycling some of its images (or what we think are its images), and on his interest in up-to-date technologies and modes of mediation (given his obvious debts to the machines on which he relies and to whose vocabularies he cannot help but subscribe). Yet there is nonetheless a *minus* that is glossed over in this reading. That minus is why Guyton's recent monochromes are not send-ups of—or even ironic commentaries on—finitude, despite their seeming courtship of degree zero. (Like the Neutral, Miller's minus takes its pleasure from being generatively deficient: Barthes calls pluses and minuses "intensive degrees.") They are, akin to Miller's dingy "masterpiece," scrubbed back down to

basics while still having clearly been put through the ringer.
Not pristine or even simply ostensible, they take their
place within the narrative of "painting," understanding that
to deny doing so would be bad faith. Scratched, scumbled,
in some instances stepped on, they are at once vaguely
expressionistic in tone, elegiac in their relation to their
(presumed) lineage, and, frankly, also a little the worse
for wear.

But there is another way to think about this lenticular
affect, this display of wear and tear that looks melancholic
from one angle and parodic from another. One thing that
is displaced (one might even say denied) in interpretations
of Guyton's work that focus on the precedents, or on the
technology and the process, is desire. To really look squarely
at this artist's work is to find desire staring you in the
face—"outplaying itself," Barthes might say, which means
desire is not locatable in the image, exactly, but is still felt
within its nimbus. Desire largely proceeds, as Lacan and
Louis Vuitton know equally well, according to what one does
not have, by making objects and ideas (and even oneself) into
what they are not.[11]

Guyton's usurpations and representations of images
—actual and "types"— proceed quite blatantly in this vein,
a now-you-see-it-now-you-don't admission that he is only
partially delivering the goods. The negotiation gives rise
to funny, queer, unexpectedly campy side effects, which are
present in all the works, but more evident in some. Take
the posters Guyton creates to announce his exhibitions.
The one for his 2006 show at West London Projects—an
elegantly composed installation of "X" paintings—uses an
image likely pulled from some cheesy soft-core site, a beefy,
hairy guy cropped at the neck and thighs, his thick torso
giving what is precisely the "wrong impression" of what was
to be shown at the gallery. Similarly, Guyton's poster for a
solo show in 2007 at Galerie Francesca Pia, in Zurich, handed
over its entire surface to the pampered visage of an anonymous 1970s fitness hunk, his face coated in a thick—vaguely
scatological—mud mask, his eyes soft with performed
relaxation. If this content seems utterly incompatible with
the rest, which seems so general—or so specific—as to resist
the kind of reading suggested, it is important to remember
just how many of Guyton's drawings and paintings are given

over to literally "flaming" effects and, less literally, how his entire practice is predicated on questions about "passing."

Susan Sontag, of course, had the last word on camp even when she first articulated it, in 1964. As she explained and as we all know well by now, camp traffics in exaggeration, in the "off," in "things-being-what-they-are-not." Less rehearsed, but even more pointedly relevant here, is another of Sontag's arguments: Camp is the purview of "style," of, therefore, the "ostensible": "To emphasize style is to slight content, or to introduce an attitude which is neutral with respect to content. It goes without saying that the Camp sensibility is disengaged, depoliticized—or at least apolitical."[12] But this attitude, which is neutral with respect to content is, she goes on to say at the essay's very end, "a tender feeling." Perhaps the question of where to place Guyton's practice in the field of contemporary art is only answered, then, by taking seriously the kind of neutrality that Barthes—and I think Sontag, too—marks as "active." So to begin again, just who does Guyton think he is? A better question might be, How does he go on, when every image looks like it will be the last? Driven by no motor other than desire.

[1] Douglas Crimp, "The End of Painting," *October* 16 (Spring 1981). Reprinted in Crimp, *On the Museum's Ruins*, MIT Press, Cambridge, Massachusetts 1993, p. 84–105. Crimp's essay specifically addresses Barbara Rose's review of the show *Eight Contemporary Artists*, held at MoMA in 1974, which included Buren. For Rose, Buren stood as emblematic of a group whose overly political aspirations bred "disenchanted, demoralized artists" producing mediocre work. In 1979, Rose curated an exhibition at the Grey Art Gallery in New York titled *American Painting: The Eighties*. Crimp argues that the show was meant as retaliation against Conceptual practices such as Buren's and aimed to reinscribe traditional ideas about the legacies of painting.

[2] From Daniel Buren, *Reboundings: An Essay*, trans. Philippe Hunt, Daled & Gevaert, Brussels 1977. Cited in Crimp, p. 103.

[3] This folding of the canvas—with the result that paintings can double in size—began well before Guyton's monochromes, manifesting in paintings that include "X"s, flames, etc., so the "navel" is itself not unique to this most recent series. However, while the "X"s and flames resulted from one large file being split in half (and thus printed in two sections, one on each side of the canvas), the monochromes are in fact the result of two iterations of the same bigblack.tif file printed one after the other.

[4] See on this topic, for instance, Benjamin H. D. Buchloh, who has long written on Buren and Buren's reception, "The Group That Was (Not) One: Daniel Buren and BMPT," in *Artforum* (May 2008), p. 310–313. He writes succinctly there: "It will be one of the questions for our decade to ponder why the spaces and practices of contestation and critique that Buren (and Hans Haacke, Michael Asher, Marcel Broodthaers, et al.) opened at the end of the '60s were—or so it seems now, at least—irredeemably hijacked."

[5] From Roland Barthes, *The Neutral*, trans. Rosalind E. Krauss and Denis Hollier, Columbia University Press, New York 2005, p. 48–49.

[6] The seminar, *Le Neutre*, was not compiled and published in France until 2002; it was subsequently translated into English in 2005.

[7] Questions regarding the relationship between one's politics and one's practice have long been asked. An interesting article appeared in *Artforum* (November 1977, p. 46–53) by Moira Roth, whose "The Aesthetic of Indifference" looked closely at "cool" practices by Duchamp, Cage, Cunningham, Rauschenberg, and Johns. Roth argues that though their practices do not comment directly on the Cold War during which they thrived, they, like "others of a more liberal and self-critical persuasion, found themselves paralyzed when called upon to act on their convictions, and this paralysis frequently appeared as indifference." I am arguing not for a paralyzing indifference, but instead for a kind of personal, even amorous politics, and it is interesting that there is similarity when it comes to how and even whether signs of the political are perceived.

[8] This is Thomas Clerc's phrase, in his preface to *The Neutral*, xxiii. Clerc is referring explicitly to the way in which Barthes uses such a wide array of sources from all areas of culture. He similarly discusses the wide net of Barthes's inquires and citations as proceeding by way of a kind of "secondhand erudition" and a "joyous dilettantism," neither of which undermines Barthes's rigor as a thinker, but both of which do highlight the unconventional nature of his method.

[9] See Bettina Funcke's 2006 essay "The Risk of Images," which focuses on Guyton's work and is included in the catalogue *Guyton, Price, Smith, Walker*, 38th Street Publishers, New York 2008. There she writes provocatively, "It remains to be seen what the appropriate response of artists will be to a new and particular risk of images. The zero dimension of the digital gives the power to manipulate to both the politician and the artist, to the terrorist and the activist, to popular culture and its critique, alike."

[10] Henry Miller, *Black Spring*, Grove Press, New York 1963, p. 57–76.

[11] Guyton takes up the question of desire as it pertains to commercial goods and advertising somewhat differently in his work for Guyton\Walker, his collaboration with artist Kelley Walker. Utilizing materials including the logo and marketing slogans for Ketel One vodka, Guyton\Walker takes up more overtly the address of cultural signs. Walker, in his solo work, can also, as Scott Rothkopf argues, be read through the logic of desire, though this is a desire thoroughly vetted—even produced—by the machinations of popular culture. See Rothkopf's essay in *Kelley Walker*, exh. cat., Le Magasin—Centre National d'Art Contemporain, Grenoble/JRP|Ringier, Zurich 2007, p. 105–125. In addition, for a valuable discussion of Guyton's work—and, more specifically, working procedures—see Rothkopf's "Modern Pictures," in *Wade Guyton: Color, Power & Style*, exh. cat., Kunstverein in Hamburg/Walther König, Cologne 2006, p. 64–83. Also, see my "Such Uneventful Events: The Work of Wade Guyton," in *Formalism. Modern Art, Today*, exh. cat., Kunstverein in Hamburg/Hatje Cantz, Berlin 2004, p. 54–61, reproduced here p. 30–35.

[12] Susan Sontag, "Notes on 'Camp'" (1964), in Sontag, *Against Interpretation and Other Essays*, Farrar, Straus and Giroux, New York 1966, p. 275–292.

100%
John Kelsey

Published in *Rich Texts: Selected Writing for Art*, Daniel Birnbaum and Isabelle Graw (ed.), Institut für Kunstkritik, Hochschule für Bildende Künste, Städelschule, Frankfurt am Main/Sternberg Press, Berlin 2010, p. 15–22. This text was commissioned for *Wade Guyton: Black Paintings*, JRP|Ringier, Zurich 2011.

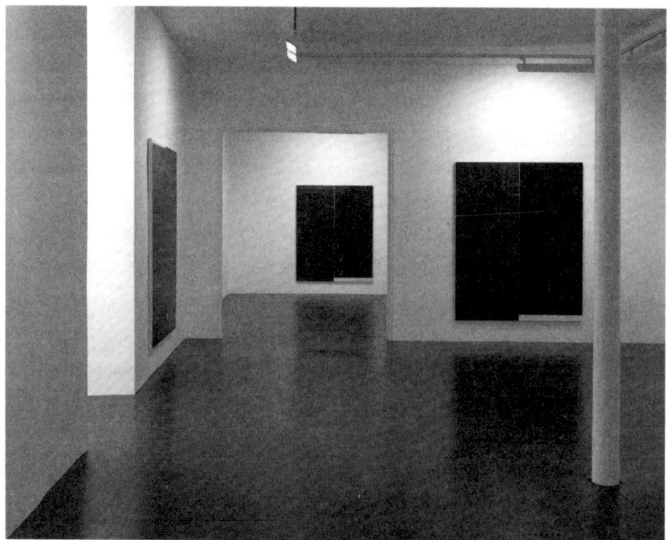

View of the exhibition *Wade Guyton*, Galerie Chantal Crousel, Paris, 2008

How much of the painting is already in the TIFF? And in the end, after the file has been selected and commanded to print, how much actually comes out of the Epson? Where does painting go when it is sent and received like this—as a *code*? The work of art seems to go outside of itself when it decides to picture the weightless, groundless, dimensionless, and genderless qualities of information, in the cybernetic sense; or when the image itself assumes such qualities in order to experience how abstraction happens today. The first thing the work abandons is the *act* of painting, and with it manual space. Replacing the "diagram" with the program or code, painting suddenly leaves the ground and approaches something like a post-Fordist condition of abstraction. Now the space of the work is no longer either optical or manual, but communicational, extending itself along a network that links one apparatus to another. The object

in the gallery is now like a hard copy or alias of the source
file on the drive, and what we are looking at is perhaps less
a painting than a "rendering." What this work displays is
the difference between sending information and receiving
aesthetic objects in the gallery, or what happens when
"black" moves from desktop to printer to museum, and
whatever is lost along the way. The monochrome is a record
of a circulation. As it is copied and communicated, discrepancies are produced. And these are what now stand in
for painting.

We are no longer experiencing painting as a relation
between a manual diagram and an optical catastrophe, which
was how Gilles Deleuze theorized the practices of Jackson
Pollock and others.[1] If diagrammatic abstraction was linked
to the work of the hand and to the introduction of a sort of
blindness within the visual order, programmatic abstraction
is more about the displacement or neutralization of the
painterly act itself. And where the diagram produced blindness and visual violence, the program only functions,
displaying the hands-off violence of design, perhaps, or
something like designer violence. Instead of blindness, there
is now only the possibility of interrupting communication.
Painting is either on or off.

Printing out mailing-address labels might be something like degree-zero painting in a world still coming
to terms with the increasing loss of distinction between the
production of art objects and the daily labor of communication. "Print" is an action selected from a menu; nobody
actually performs it. The rest—the printing, the painting—
is mostly automatic: a connection between the design
program and the printing apparatus has been okayed as the
artist manages and monitors his production from the side.
This could even be a definition of contemporary art: an
encounter with our own absence in the middle of the very
activities we manage and monitor. Such encounters also
involve a reckoning with the ways in which we ourselves are
inhabited and even predicted by the readymade programs
whose users we say we are.[2] Most of the time, we do not
realize how *activated* we have become as artists and users.
The monochrome is a means of displaying this. At the same
time, it can be a way of reducing to a minimum the degree
of our activation in the middle of communication. In this

case, the monochrome signals the creative subject's possible deactivation, or even a disconnection, from the program of painting. If the "blank" TIFF (who would still call this rectangle a "field"?) is still related to the painterly blank, the former no longer pretends to be anything less than 100% information. It is this 100% that also now stands in for the act of painting.

For the eye that still inhabits the modern spaces of literature and painting, and that scans pages and walls for sense and sensation, the monochrome is the image of a radical minimum. It is a spiritual or ascetic void, a pictorial purification. But in the discursive or "connexionist" space, where work and life now lose their difference, 100% black is the *most* a machine or an artist can say, do, or send, a total saturation and total activation of the space of communication. Here, black may still stand for a minimum, but from the angle of function or performance, it is a maximum. If Mallarmé were still here, he might say that black is the full dress of sense (and its shadow too), the formal attire of every possible transmission.

On the contemporary screen, where writing, too, finds its image, black is the color of "automatic." It is what 100% looks like. Here, in the visual space that writing now shares with design and communication, black is both a kind of information and a means of informing. When it is not selected, it is the default color of anything we do or send, including literature. Here, writing and painting are no longer so much about spilling ink, but about managing shades, sizes, styles and quantities of information. And writers and painters have never been so neighborly: they share the same screens and the same postures. Already the canvas—like a Rorschach—starts to resemble the sequenced pages of a book, with a seam or margin (some say "zip") down its middle. It is a picture of information without a message, a post-literary document. It is also a sort of shadow painting of the TIFF it was composed with.

Do graphics exist? The "painting" commands the wall and the room, but its source file is only a few compressed kilobytes of code. And just as the designer fills in a rectangular box with what is referred to as "#000000" (or black) in the invisible source code of a digital "page," Wade Guyton has filled or blackened exhibition spaces in New York, Paris, and Frankfurt. These three shows are like one show repeated or communicated between the three cities. The filling in of digital windows is followed by the distribution of ink across canvases, and then by the ritual installing and staging of black in the galleries. In order to show itself here, communication becomes decor.

But the TIFF is nothing in itself. It only really exists or becomes visible through use, or when one device communicates it to another. It is much less than an idea, and much more efficient. A means of circulating information between two or more machines or galleries in a network, the TIFF, we could say, is potential communication, the pure possibility of transit, which in Guyton's case is used to send "black" from hard drive to printer to canvas to wall. Black is circulated and also at a strange standstill in the paintings and in the gallery. Here, the installation produces an optical rhythm that departs from the painterly dance of the diagram in order to approach the on/off, on/off of the program. This binary pattern will sometimes produce effects reminiscent of Bridget Riley's Op art.

In the gallery, a false floor of black plywood introduces a material hollow beneath the viewers' feet. It is a strange feeling to realize that one is standing in the same space as information, as if formatted along with it, a body dragged and dropped in a room full of ink. It is the same in the city, when we transmit ourselves through the urban program of Manhattan. We say we are like tourists here, but we are also like files on the move, opening and closing, constantly updating and duplicating ourselves. Under our feet, the hollow, flimsy feeling of a stage renders the body strangely present in the act of scanning the show. And this feeling is accompanied by a perception of how completely absent the body has become in the paintings.

The gallery is no longer a theater of human activity or even passivity, but an activated space where information, bodies, and money are rapidly circulated, and where this power of circulation is momentarily frozen in images and objects. In other words, the canvases on view are not so much finished, final things, as they are a series of interrupted movements. These are abstractions torn from and at the same time irretrievably lodged in a condition of productive mobilization. And in its interruption, "painting," too, is put at a strange, fresh distance. The blankness that surrounds us here is both "on" and "off," and is perhaps working on a third possibility in the relation between the two.

Because their surfaces expose information dropouts and discrepancies between source image and printout, we could say these paintings are failed attempts at picturing TIFFs, a serial repetition of this. Often, a canvas is over-printed multiple times so that several copies occupy a single surface, overloading it. But no matter how awash in ink they are, these images will never achieve the thickness of painting. And we wonder if the Epson is even capable of failing the way a painting can.

Connoisseurs will insist on the many subtle and unpredicted differences produced by the Epson's struggling printer heads, mechanical glitches, and even the rough traces of the studio floor on the canvas' sensitive surface. As if whatever escapes the program is now painting. As if painting occurred finally as information dropout (or over-load), as mechanical malfunction. These minor traffic accidents are what produce images of transit and transmis-sion: they make us see the TIFF in the room precisely because it never finally arrived here. And 100% black is a way of displaying the fact that the artist and his gestures have already exited the space and the moment of the picture's production. We are in a sort of shadowland of painting.

In a way, Guyton is dragging and dropping these shows into New York, Paris, and Frankfurt. We get the feel-ing that the spaces he fills have in the meantime abandoned the possibility of experience, that they are more like maga-zine pages than rooms. At an opening, bodies circulate against walls of TIFFs, and we remember that Warhol's shadow paintings were used as a backdrop for fashion shoots, and that his wallpapers, films, and publishing ventures were also means of displaying the being-in-mediation of postindustrial, post-Expressionist bodies. Against such backdrops, Warhol elaborated a real style of disappearance, or disappearance as a style of use. Guyton's updated decor, on the other hand, stages the productive relation between communication and appearance: work is not what we do, but how we show up, like on a screen. Making the Epson struggle, the artist causes a sort of material stammering within the program, putting communication in closer proximity to interruption. It is a stammering of the Epson and also of painting.

The monochrome is a document that tells us of nothing but its own circulation, presenting the pure possibility of communication by a possible artist. And if the artist no longer locates himself in manual space, if the picture is automatic, then the painter is somewhere out here on the floor with us, another dislocation. Here is where black is momentarily extracted from its program, casting a shadow that is as good-looking as Kasimir Malevich and Calvin Klein.

The contemporary artist's productive displacement is constantly encountering its own image—also like a shadow—on the screen, on the wall, and on the page. So if the artist, as he works, is already producing images of communication, he must find ways of intervening exactly there, in this space and moment where displacement becomes appearance. In this way—by working on both the distribution and display of information—he can perhaps begin to recover what Giorgio Agamben has called the "gestural sphere."[3] How can we picture and interrupt our own endless transmission within the networked spaces we inhabit and extend today? The monochrome can be taken up as a means of reappropriating everything that already disappears us in the middle of our productive activities. On the one hand, the Epson is exploited to produce the feeling of an easy, convincing, institutional decor. On the other hand, this decor is a direct occupation of discursive space, returning the possibility of use. And if the painter prefers not to show up here, the user—his double—is already working overtime.

Not long ago, Guyton was printing over other artists' images, using pages torn from catalogues and the back issues of art magazines. Sending these pages through a desktop printer, interrupting them with his programmed marks, Guyton intervened directly within the mediation of artistic practice, discourse, and value. Taken up as a pure means, employed as a discursive and material support, the magazine or catalogue became a display system for new and possible gestures. And as the painter or printer elaborates ways of using that somehow remain out of reach or blind to the author, he also learns to displace himself with a strange ease between discourse and design, communication and image. This ease is accompanied by a certain indifference to the ownership of messages and signatures. It also involves simply letting the program function. The artist intervenes where the production of communication by means of communication happens, in the black of the font and in the sending of the image, outputting paintings like pages, and putting transmission on display.

[1] Gilles Deleuze, "The Diagram," *The Deleuze Reader*,
Columbia University Press, New York 1993, p. 193–200.
[2] Vilém Flusser, *Towards a Philosophy of Photography*, Reaktion
Books, London 2000. In theorizing an emergent
postindustrial era in terms of a shift from a text-based to
an image-based culture, Flusser proposes that the
photographer is, first of all, already a function of the
camera's program.
[3] Giorgio Agamben, "Notes On Gesture," in *Infancy and
History: On the Destruction of Experience*, Verso, London 2007,
p. 150.

Man and Machine:
A Wade Guyton Retrospective
Peter Schjeldahl

Originally published in *The New Yorker*, "The Art World" column, October 15, 2012, p. 94–95.

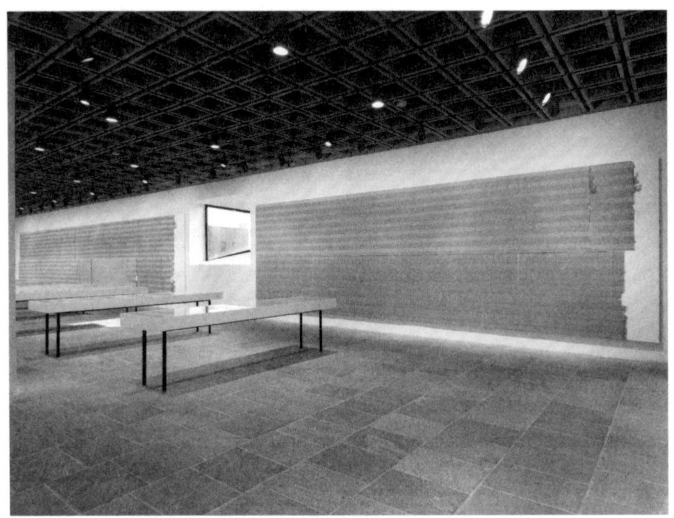

View of the exhibition *OS*, Whitney Museum of American Art, New York, 2012

The still early career of the American artist Wade Guyton has starred a trio of gadgets. They are the small, medium, and very large ink-jet printers with which he strangely rejuvenates the aesthetic philosophy, and the dramatic beauty, of classical abstract painting. A terrific new survey of his work at the Whitney Museum includes sculptures and installations, but the pictorial works dominate. These are not really paintings or drawings: they are canvas swaths or pages torn from books and magazines which have been forced through the printers, acquiring overlays of Guyton's rudimentary digital designs—from a repertoire of shapes, lines, stripes, and typed "X"s or "U"s—and incurring smears, stutters, registration errors, and other happy glitches. But they sure look like paintings and drawings, ranging in style from busily geometric to near-monochrome black. Stretched or framed, they evoke the noble rawness of a

Pollock or a Rothko. The work is ingenious, and also moving, as a counterattack of the spirit on a culture whose proliferating technical means, by eclipsing the handmade, disembody imagination. By making machines do lovely things that they were not designed to do, Guyton scores comeback goals for primitive wonder.

Guyton was born in Hammond, Indiana, in 1972, and grew up in the small town of Lake City, Tennessee. His father, who died when Guyton was two, and his stepfather, also deceased, were both steelworkers. Guyton's mother, a homemaker, sometimes worked as a secretary at the Catholic Church the family attended. As a child, Guyton was so uninterested in art, he has said, that he was pleased to have his stepfather do his elementary-school drawing homework for him. That changed while he was a student at the University of Tennessee, by way of intellectual excitement: the early 1990s were a heyday of academic critical theory, when thinking skeptically about art could seem as good as, if not better than, making it. The artists who counted were image-recycling gravediggers of tradition, chiefly the Pictures Generation of Cindy Sherman, Sherrie Levine, and Richard Prince. A prevailing scorn for handcraft encouraged Guyton, who readily confesses his own manual ineptitude. But something dramatic happened in the circle of his artist friends at the university, which included two others who became successful, Kelley Walker and Meredyth Sparks: they decided that the grandparents were cool. It often happens that, in youth, we glamorize a past that our immediate elders tell us is over and done. So it was with Guyton and his peers.

Guyton came to New York in 1996. Twice rejected for admission to the Whitney Independent Study Program, which was at the time a virtual think tank of critical theory, he attended Hunter College. There he studied under the formerly minimalist, always inventive sculptor Robert Morris. Guyton also became immersed in the art world while working for seven years as a guard at the solemnly avant-gardish Dia Art Foundation. His early New York work—sculpture (most of which he later destroyed) and photographs of architecture—was minimalism redux. A recreated example at the Whitney show is *Inverted Woodpile* (2002/2012), a leaning stack of scrap lumber that Guyton found on the street and simply turned upside down. Since 2004, he has continued to fashion sculpture, in a series of fat, mirrored stainless steel "U"s in various heights. They are pleasant enough, but I cannot imagine what, except perhaps market demand, keeps them coming. For me, they provide only trace elements of the formal and imaginative tensions that inform Guyton's achievements in two dimensions.

In 2002, frustrated, he has said, by his failure at drawing, Guyton hit on using his computer, scanner, and printer to alter pages from old art and design publications. In the show, scores of the results are hung on walls or arrayed on blue vinyl tiles in a row of handsome display cases. There are vaguely Constructivist geometric shapes, the inevitable "X"s, and random-seeming blotches overlaid on images of modern architecture and, occasionally, on the works of Goya, Ensor, or other Expressionist masters. The gentle vandalism stirs poetic qualities of yearning in and for the orphaned material. Stick with it. The emotional reward is a gradual simmer.

Guyton is a bibliophile, though not an especially discerning one. The edges of some spectacular works on canvas from 2006 that feature scanned images of flames reveal their source: the beat-up cover of a book, minus the title and the author's name. A stern superego of rigorous taste, instilled by Guyton's academic training, keeps his art's apparent attitude distanced and cool. His passions sneak up on you and, when they take hold, can feel like your own —as if, at a formal social event, you found yourself suddenly and awkwardly in love with the host. There is a remarkably civilized lightness about the experience, which transcends the familiar winks and nudges of complicity that are found in so much only-too-well-schooled contemporary art. Rather, there is the ardor of a connoisseur who hopes to convert you to his vision, but is too respectful of both you and himself to impose a hard sell.

In 2004, Guyton decided that what worked as a surrogate for drawing might serve for painting, too. Experimentation led to several series on primed linen canvas. Large works—the topper being a 50-foot-long pattern of red and green stripes, blown up from the endpapers of an Italian design catalogue—are made by folding canvases, as tall as nine feet, in half horizontally and sending them through his biggest printer twice. The machine's struggles with the unwieldy cloth produce glories of textural incident that recall the imperfections in Andy Warhol's silk screens. Warhol looms large for Guyton, as for artists who deal with issues of image reproduction. So may Gerhard Richter, the German master of painterly blurs, whose new show of computer-derived prints, at the Marian Goodman Gallery, makes for a chance tag team, with Guyton, of artists who are 40 years apart in age. Both address the historic task, urgent in art today, of coming to sensible and sensitive terms with the global juggernaut of the digital medium.

Guyton hardly accepts every result of his process. He rejects many, he told me when I met him at the Whitney. He added that recent advances in technology pose a threat of too much sophistication. "They're getting smarter," he complained of the printers. To make gray pictures, for example, he must take tortuous measures to disable his newest printer's insistence that black is a combination of nine colors. With a mental squint, I heard him talking about his high-tech gear in a tone like that of painters discussing paints and brushes—always a sure sign of maturity in a new medium. Most computer-generated art to date has been marred by a tedious infatuation with novel effects, which turn passé in a twinkling. With Guyton, the electronic becomes a class of workaday studio tools.

The show, as installed by the artist in collaboration with the Whitney curator Scott Rothkopf, is an over-all artwork in itself. An arrangement of temporary walls creates a palimpsest of visual echoes and comparisons, affirming Guyton's temperamental forte as a critical assessor of his own production. He visually footnotes his sensibility by including in the show a row of five tubular-steel Cesca chairs, designed by Marcel Breuer in 1928. Breuer, the architect of the Whitney building, has long fascinated Guyton. A wall text states that these specific chairs, upholstered in sickly decorator colors, once belonged to the Enron Corporation. I do not know what to do with that fact, but it is charged with something. Also on view is the frame of a Cesca chair which, in 2001, Guyton wrestled by hand into a free-form sculpture. The work is no great shakes, but its burlesque of a love–hate, Oedipal struggle with the modern tradition signals Guyton's ambition. He wants nothing less than to weave the art-historical past, as a challenging presence, into art's emerging future. Perilously, he is a leader.

Idylls of a Chosen XXXXXX
Boško Blagojević and Sam Pulitzer

Originally published in Yilmaz Dziewior (ed.), *Wade Guyton, Guyton\Walker, Kelley Walker*, exh. cat., Kunsthaus, Bregenz/Walther König, Cologne 2012, p. 95–99.

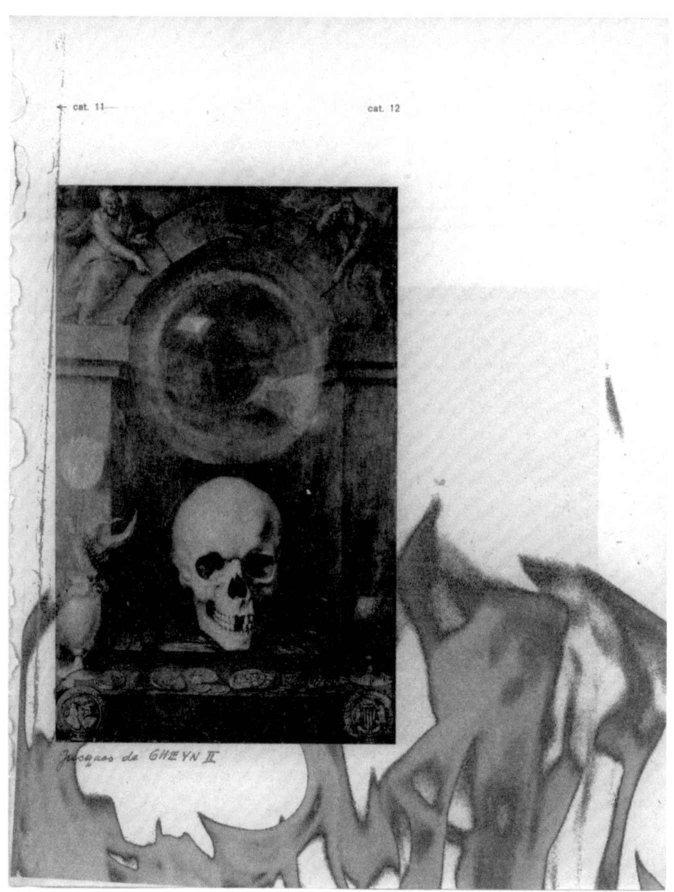

Untitled (cat. 11 cat. 12), 2008
Epson DURABrite inkjet on book page, 24.8 × 19.1 cm

Carcass U

What is it like to live in the carcass
of a leviathan? To dwell among
the canopies of its skin, buttressed
by bone, to make a carnival of the
flesh and gore of its brethren behe-
moth? Does one look above to see
the palaces of heaven, stone-like
with the colors of soot and ash in
this time to come, as the messiah
indulges now in this terrestrial
feast of complete ends and zilch
means?

Forfeiting their ostensible
abstraction it is easy to mistake a
number of Wade Guyton's canvas
works for an image that depicts
the destruction of the World Trade
Towers—two stark columns consumed with flame with a cascade
of "U"s falling victim to gravity and
rendered with the poetry of a bad
fax. This is of course a stupid thing
to do, identifying pictures in matter-
of-fact patches of pigment. And it
is even more idiotic to think of the
now absent towers as a leviathan

whose carcass has been skinned to resituate the feast of the
messiah's governing loves across the howling sepulcher of
this event. But if intelligence was the apocalyptic meat, who
hoards all the smarts? Who are the poor dogs at the table
lucky enough to crack a bone for a hint of marrow? And what
is the critical reception of Wade's work if not but a banquet
of so many riches? Perhaps this is why I am choosing marrow
with a dog's dumb palette. Is it that I am late to the hall?
Why I elect to see towers ablaze in striated rectangles like a
moron unable to compute the fuzzy play of these matter-of-
fact images … And elsewhere I will gnaw into the staccato
of glitch "X"s as if they were windmills of bone peppering the
atmosphere with the dust of its gargantuan rot. Many meals
have been served in the course of the lives of these images,
with the stagger at which these towers tumble deadpan
out of a printer and into the hands of Wade and his staff.
Loud meals swallowed whole, these technical surfaces and
subsequent extrusion into the phenomena known as objects
are gnashed up for others as if they had to vomit a witch's
tea leaves into the famished mouths of its young. What
if there was nothing to know of these works, only a pretext
through which things subsist? That maybe only they are
refugees, in which a number have dwelled, springs into which
some have cured their dyspeptic ills, foxholes into which
one may wantonly crawl. There is nothing that this sapiential
idiot wants to explicate—there is prolly nothing that it can,
its brain is the size of a pea and thinks with its jaw. It merely
craves something in its mouth. Inane pipings of a feral
esophagus ledgered over the sensible harmonics of writing
dancing to a fucking tune—a clone, a d-clone, that bad
fax orchestrated to the grinding of the spheres, yeah that
dumb 7"—"noise not music" …

Just Scrolling

Towers fall, but failing away is not the same as disappearing.
Fortunately, we no longer have to bow to our knees before
statues of gods. But we bow our knees, if only in fantasy,
before many other things that hang over us or hold us down,
that "look at" us or leave us stunned. As we know, Benjamin
writes of the "decline of the aura" in the modern age, but
for him, "decline" does not mean disappearance. Rather,

it means, as in the Latin declination—moving downward, inclining, deviating, or inflecting in a new way. Falling is not the same as disappearing, and neither is the downward scrolling motion of an exhibition mediated through the backlit something or other. When we look at an exhibition by Wade Guyton, it is important to know in which direction we are moving through it. So where to start chewing?

The wolves are at the door. Or is it that all those already inside have succumbed to lunar fever and its lupine calling? Should I just proceed from this desire, or express it instead as a training, a learning that this jaw must undergo through its coldcocked deprivation? When the sky is dulled by the rain of heaven's ash, who would not want to be out cracking bones for their putty meat? Strip mining the world of things of significance in favor of mere subsistence; chomping away at reality's clothes to rend asunder paltry nudities as digestible parcels? Compressing data … lol no. Zero concentration … A cybernetic mutt … Moving its dumb skull from screen to screen like an obedient cunt trained to hunt through the flesh of informatic surfaces for bones of quality gnaw … A hound dumb to the ambergris yanked from the depths of the gored leviathan to sweeten the necks and wrists of the righteous from the suffused pestilences of history's decay.

The leviathan's flesh can be printed. Its bones extruded, fabricated like some necessary organ. Naturally the end of days is not bad at all as nature holds no revelations. (Rather nature is ground onto which chicken bones and tealeaves may be portentously cast.) Instead, laid out on the table is what is all that remains, towering infernos parceled out in morsel form. Books burned since brains do not amount to shit anymore, knowledge signaled instead in the windfallen tracings of sparkling embers, pinpointing all those other skulls possessed with cravings for whatever flesh can still be produced—beyond cops and beyond god, the technics of flesh are knotted, clotted, and spliced together like the threads of providence spun not by three norse hags, but by a skeletal congress possessed by lupine appetites. A quick look to the fairytales of modern industry that tells of man succeeding for the first time in making the product of his past, dead labor operates on a large scale gratuitously as if a force of nature, where the phenomenon of life itself is a production of a crucible of sepulchral technics. To refrain, nature holds no revelations. And that is especially the case for a being without a brain, it is a femur to complete a leg, a wart to complete a toad, a gasket to complete an engine, a mere appendage to an already existing material condition of production. Bone bodies in the mausoleum of time, housing themselves in the kinda sorta human drapery of their messianic meals playing out Turing experiments within the false dialectic of living and dead (labor, the congealed bone dust and gastric putty that makes the working day that much more expedient for the living by concretizing times passed into the instruments of fixed capital) until the cows come home.

Actual Plan

Is there anguish in me as I write this? Is it the cocaine in my nose? The alcohol in my liver? The black bile clogging the pathways of my holistic spirit? Are these words a losing of one's way into necropolis, of tripping over one's feet in the blackened guts of a whale run ashore by the ending of days. What is another day in eternity? What is another day in eternity when dwelling has the agency of carrion and creation is a by-product of surviving? Surviving, that is promoting the consensual hallucination that one is alive even as a computer prints out the flesh that drapes your bones and that is stretched to build your house, that homologizes a body's wicked technics to the physics of grass, deer, orphans, uranium, and all of god's blessed little footlings. As if to say, same shit, same sound system sex appeal (no to the organic-inorganic disjunction), different circuitry only. How can a black box be put to use in a heap of peaceable wreckage? When heaven has forfeited its distinction from all else, what to do with all the leftover subroutines that once elevated souls evermore? Turned into food, "X"s and "U"s to state hungover souls, alpha-numerics slow roasted by flame to some epicurean delicacy, word morsels that communicate nothing but their sensual potentiality. I mean, when heaven has burned, what else is there to do but savor all these once-heralded carcasses that float like angel cakes down to our festive mouths?

    A descriptive wall label recent to the moment of writing this text pointed out the interpellative innuendo

of Guyton's use of the letter U—that these canvas-rested
or Robert Watts-esque mirrored chromed artworks point the
finger at you in much like those found at the receiving end
of those impatient fingertips tapping away SMS messages.
Perhaps it was hinted at elsewhere alongside another accompanying wall label, but let us calm down and forget these
"X"s as ragged windmills for the time being, and think of
their situation in personal mobile devices, which of course
turn them into kisses. Of course that is magical thinking,
dog thought there. Naturally they are substitutions for kisses,
but I am romantic, and when I type them I really mean it
like the silly song *Kiss Me Thru the Phone*. But again, it is a
really animal relationship to technology—a dog sticks its
tongue in the receiver, it falls into some portal that takes it
miles away to the other end. Perhaps if I were to stand up
upright on my hind legs for long enough I would be able to
understand this as the *amor fati* of dead labor, some simu-
lacral connectivity that has no choice but to be affirmed so
as to lay the bed for pleasure and all its fissure flower given
its affordances by communicative media. As the laboring
lives of yore are pressed into the technical potential of the
present, leeched forth as contemporary for the purpose
of preserving its yield (drawings …) all these graceful appa-
ratuses join into a daisy chain of mutual crotch sniffing.

Stochastic Couch machine

The aura once imposed in religious images now supposed
in artists' studios is hard to see, so try instead and follow
your nose. The aurel aura, a cute sort of alliteration at this
point if nothing else, the smell of a teenage bedroom:
I mean of course the smell of spilled seed, semen—a thing
sometimes evocative of chlorine (depending on diet) that
is neither clean nor completely putrid. It is the smell of sex
when sex has not happened. The body's chemistry responds
differently to porn and manual stimulation than the higher-
stakes and performance game of working with or against
someone. Wade works alone in that sense. The smell seems
to always indicate the presence of the computer, the
machine. Is this not the horny stink of the so-called new
economy? If you want to find the keyboard, follow your
nose. It is one of the enduring shames of my private life,

but I know I am not alone here. Which brings me to another
point ...

Why so much rhythmic repetition in this carnival?
Maybe because, like a breath, something about Wade's work
passes through, infiltrates, mixes with, permeates, and dis-
integrates any certainty about space. This something is
again the aura, which we must not understand in terms of a
third characteristic, but rather which returns to the most
archaic and "physical," the most material sense of the word
aura. This meaning is that of breath, of the air that surrounds
us as a subtle, moving, absolute place, the air that permeates
us and makes us breathe. However outrageously immaterial
or effortless Wade's efforts in the studio are presented as
(by curators who may still for the next few years seem radical
to their more easily-spoken peers), the depression key on
a keyboard, like a piston—like breath (!) again—is a fairly
impotent act in the singular sense. Before every idiot was
hacking away at a laptop at home and work, world power
could be said to be symbolized by the image of the big red
button: a menacing symbol that when pushed could release a
battery of ICBMs to microwave cities, populations, whatever.
It is a fun fantasy that mistakes the collective clattering of
many for a mythical single coming (orgasm)—that we never
quite achieve. Orgasms are little deaths after all because they
cannot seem to keep us away from the next. Time passes,
and you need to push again. All of this to say: a single canvas
by Wade simply cannot stand alone. You do not really own a
Guyton unless you have two. Likewise, the depression of a
button—described famously in other writings on his works
as the sole generator of the "U" or "X"—toys with the idea
of ease or effortlessness with the same menacing cruelty of a
cat playing with some captured, disabled, still-breathing prey.

Or try this: when the artist projects his voice from the
hallowed cathedral of a ripped-off Microsoft Word, the echo
is never taken for granted quite like the architecture that
shapes it.

Multiplicity in Wade's work is also of course about
pleasure. So perhaps this pleasure could be proffered as
some reason for the appearance of asses and chiseled abs in
some of Wade's promotional posters, also not forgetting to
mention nothing of the work-safe aesthetic pleasure that
this art routinely commands?

A friend of mine wrote that autonomy is not choice you make, it is a program you follow.

He also wrote, "Were you ever asked by a tea tree to help him thru a difficult period?"

This is not to suggest that this ending of days is something that was reached by the passage of time. Not so. The messiah is never not here, the negative dialectics of never not working. And so goes the feast at his table. This terminal point of history is really the site of departure for all possible beginnings, where the scraps left on the table become a wet nurse to this whatever infancy. The hardwiring of social relations to the documentation of a superannuated barbarity. Or something …

As the documents of barbarity coagulate into the technics of a wholly functional anthropological strategy, the modular swaths of Wade's tugged spools clothe the viewing pleasure of a subject who is only residual human—subjects whose historical deliverance is brokered by the technical malfunctioning of a commercial imaging device modulated to the tune of artisanal facture. A printer the head, the artist a sticky hand pressing against a collapsed chest that has forgotten its last breath.

But let us forget these …

Preserving eternity …

Idylls of a chosen damned …

The factory is a "living mechanism"—more specifically, a "productive organism that is purely objective, in which the laborer becomes a mere appendage to an already existing material condition of Production."

Concretions of dead labor living in a corpse; why let a corpse get in the way of an orgasm. Necromantik.

Living supplement to dead labor. The tugger, the tugboat that carries the load ashore.

Bile, bile behind my eyes, oozing out through my tear ducts. Bile that perverts visions, that stupidly confuses death for life. For flesh. A vision much like the recent spate of best sellers that take old books and fill the crevices idiotically with zombies…

Sexiness is just as programmed as the output subroutines that print a painting. Inorganic sex appeal …

And of course this is just a recalcitrant hallucination, a fogged vision borne of things barely known.

Lust for the dead, for the spirits that linger in the wake of abstraction's sublimations, spirits that odor, flavor the air …

You call hunger love, and where you see nothing more, there dwell your gods. Gods? And love?

Wade Guyton:
Whitney Museum of American Art
Achim Hochdörfer

Originally published in *Artforum*, vol. 51, no. 6, February 2013, p. 234–237. Translated from German by Alexander Scrimgeour.

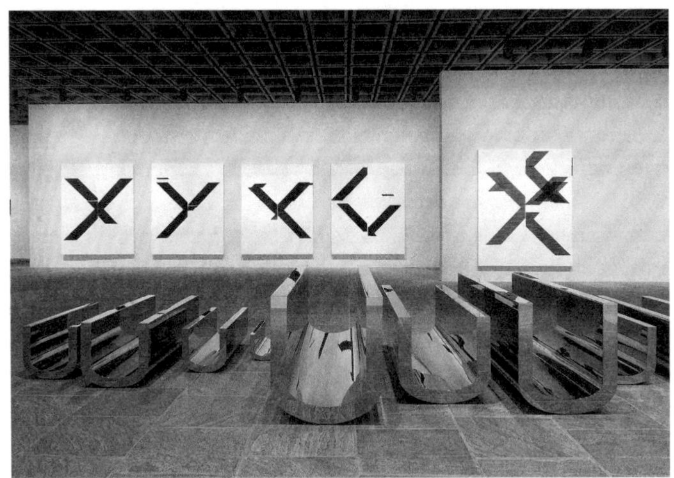

View of the exhibition *OS*, Whitney Museum of American Art, New York, 2012

The logic of the modern era
demands revolutions: decisive ruptures that enable sweeping paradigm shifts and the introduction
of new ways of seeing. In hindsight,
such ruptures can often be seen
asthe outcome of periods of transition, those interregnums that
are not dominated by a prevailing
narrative and thus allow for an
atmosphere of indeterminacy and
openness, in which antithetical
motives and genealogies can
suddenly and surprisingly be connected with one another. Jasper
Johns, for example, was buoyed by
such a historical constellation: the
speed with which his institutional
breakthrough occurred in 1958
is matched only by the difficulty
of his historical categorization to
this day. His work looks back to
one period as it looks forward
to another, and it is tied as much
to European modernism as it is to
Abstract Expressionism, Neo-
Dada, Minimalism, and Pop. This
intermeshing of various sensibilities

does not run aground in an eclectic "anything goes": in fact, nearly the opposite is true. If a dominant paradigm forfeits its position, only then do the inner historical conflicts of a time become visible in their full complexity.

Wade Guyton seems to have caught one of these fortuitous moments. His rise at the turn of the millennium accompanied the first signs of the disintegration of the critical formation of the 1990s. Around that time, artists and critics affiliated with institutional critique suddenly began to reflect on previously taboo realms such as melancholy, formalism, and affect, and the lines of battle between so-called new media, and the traditional genres of sculpture and painting came to seem less and less relevant. In Guyton's work there is a collision of models from different eras: an easy congruence of aspects of Minimalism and Pop, high modernism and commercial design, Appropriation art and strategies of institutional critique, preindustrial and post-industrial methods. Moreover, Guyton does not stage the far-reaching digitization of our world as a radical break, as do both technology's progressive apologists and its conservative critics—a fact perfectly illustrated by the purposeful super-impositions of analog and digital techniques in his works on paper. And even the "paintings" that are fed through an ink-jet printer reject simplified polarizations between the analog as mimetic, embodied, and contemplative and the digital as immaterial, dispersed, and abstract.

Indeed, at least as seen from the outside, Guyton's career has developed without a hiccup, reconciling diverse positions not only in his production but in his reception as well. He is embedded in a broad network of artist friends, critics, curators, gallerists, and collectors, and a market for his work emerged with impressive speed. He almost instan-taneously attained canonical status in universities and art schools, where he is someone against whom students are already beginning to rebel. Accordingly, a considerable burden of expectation fell on his first midcareer survey, curated by Scott Rothkopf at the Whitney Museum of American Art. The occasion raised several questions: how would Guyton's art historical elevation affect the prevailing view of this relatively young artist? Would the show live up to such high expectations? Would his work be able to pull off the balancing act between its status as a product desired

by collectors, and its critical seriousness? An explosive
mixture of enthusiasm, envy, skepticism, and sheer anticipation created a palpable tension before the opening. But
Guyton and Rothkopf were not distracted by any of this and
produced a consummately curated exhibition. There could
hardly have been a greater contrast between the art world
buzz surrounding the occasion and the serenity and concen-
trated intensity of the show itself.

Upon entering, visitors were presented with a 2006
series of pictures featuring the letter "U" amid raging flames,
as if the emptied linguistic vessels were literally being heated
up. From the beginning, Guyton seemed to want to make
clear that his work renounces the classical oppositions of
Minimalist cool and Expressionist heat, of Conceptual
semiotics and modernist pictoriality. Behind these works
lay a system of partitions, as simple as it was varied, which
faced the viewer and created an open space that offered
different sight lines and routes through the show. Parallel
partitions of various sizes were layered behind one another
and were reminiscent, as the press text suggests, of the
pages of a book as well as of the stacked windows on a
computer screen: the idea of interweaving the analog and
the digital was thus also made into a leitmotif of the exhibition design.

Examples of Guyton's early works were represented
by pieces including installments from the series "Untitled
Action Sculptures" (2001–), and a particularly beautiful
ripped canvas, *Untitled* (2004), which hung loosely on one
of the temporary walls. Elements within later works, such
as the U-shapes, migrated from sculptures to canvases
to works on paper, and various series of the already "classic"
ink-jet-printed pictures were hung on the long partitions.
Two monumental, horizontal-stripe paintings—both
Untitled (2012), and made for the occasion of the show—
covered the back wall of the gallery and functioned as a
framing device for the entire exhibition. Altogether, the
installation established a rhythm of conceptual compression
and contrapuntal subplots. Every detail of the show was
carefully considered, and yet there was still room for
surprising cadences and visual discoveries.

This alternation between series and isolated works
circled around the antagonism (so central since early

modernism) between the auratic charge generated by the singular presence of the image, and its diminution or depletion. Take, for example, *Untitled* (2008), a sequence of rectangular canvases that were hung so closely together that it was nearly impossible to differentiate between the external borders of the constituent panels and the broader connecting structure suggested by the horizontal, slightly off-register bars within the pictures. Indeed, closely related works appeared again and again in various settings throughout the space, as if proliferating, troubling the borders between individual pieces: Guyton's works on paper were in one instance hung traditionally framed on the wall, then encountered as a group in a wooden frame on the ground (*Untitled*, 2005) or lying next to one another haphazardly in vitrines (*Zeichnungen für ein grosses Bild*, 2010). Such migrations and reverberations seemed to enact visually the way we encounter images today, with their endless transposition and mobility between different scales and contexts, between screen and world, zoom and thumbnail.

The Whitney's elegant Brutalist architecture designed by Marcel Breuer, with its repetitive open-grid concrete ceiling and patterned stone floor, was extremely accommodating to Guyton's aesthetic and became another kind of frame or echo of the work. It seemed a happy coincidence that Guyton has several times included chairs designed by the museum's architect, Marcel Breuer, in his exhibitions. Indeed, the snaking metal tubing from a deconstructed Breuer chair in *Untitled Action Sculpture (Chair)* (2001), was emblematic of the artist's versatile reception of modernism, which overlays homage and estrangement, elegant functionality and eccentric (dis-)placement.

Guyton's works look as if they follow a simple set of rules. There is a "signature style," based on a process that recalls, albeit in a different historical moment, Pollock's drip technique and its dance between chance and control. Guyton enters a set of typographical elements and scanned or found images into a software program such as Photoshop or Word and then merely presses "print"—a winner every time. Yet his method cannot be understood as a gesture of genius akin to a master's brushstroke, or even as its digital equivalent; its success depends far more on the artist's conceptual framing. Guyton lays out the anchor points of the artist's endeavor in such a way that the intentional decisions and accidental effects in each stage of his process become indistinguishable. Unplanned overlaps, machine errors, and physical limitations during the printing process are as important as everything else that gives meaning to the work. Yet this kind of interweaving is more than a nullification of the distinction between the intentional and the contingent. For example, when one sees a blank gap in certain works, it often corresponds to the canvas getting caught or stopped on its way through the printer; Guyton then has to pull at the canvas to keep it going, and that pull is registered as a white space. Guyton thus also "learns" how to adjust or fix certain problems that arise in his process, while remaining leery of allowing such solutions to themselves displace the refutation of authorial gestures in his work.

What sets Guyton's work apart from the current fascination with the seductive surfaces that the digital realm makes possible is that here technological progress does not become an end in itself, nor does it masquerade as creative freedom. On the contrary, Guyton's use of digital technology is based on his systematically demanding more from it than it is able to offer. He mistreats his printer, confronts it with commands that go far beyond the limits of its potential, and feeds it information or material that it is unable to process. In this sense, Guyton's art is fundamentally physical, even expressive: its inherent conflicts are forced to the outside. Digital code manifests in his canvases in an otherwise unknown form—as moody and unmanageable; as if something were seeping out from these seemingly anonymous signs that one would never have expected there: a subjectivity that has broken free of the subject, and yet is not given over to the machine.

2008–2014
Catherine Chevalier

Originally published in *Wade Guyton: 26 avril–7 juin 2008*, exh. cat., Galerie Chantal Crousel, Paris/
Walther König, Cologne 2014, p. 67–73.

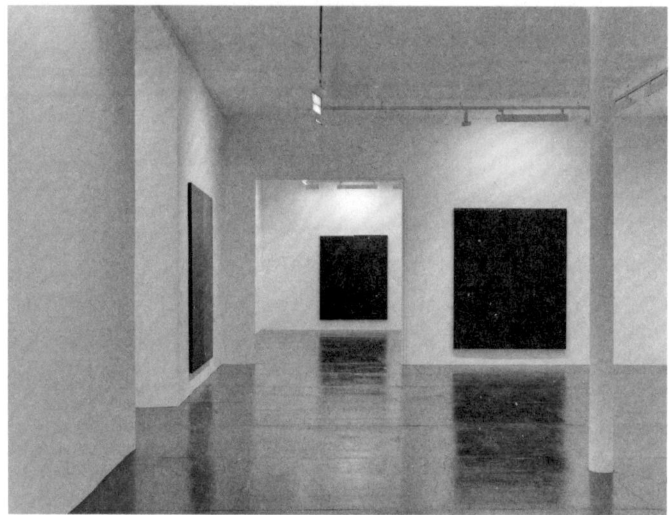

View of the exhibition *26 avril–7 juin 2008*, Galerie Chantal Crousel, Paris, 2014

For his second exhibition at Galerie Chantal Crousel, Wade Guyton presented a new series of black paintings arranged in exactly the same way as those in his first exhibition at the gallery in 2008. The canvases were produced by almost identical means in his New York studio, using the same TIFF file he had used previously, and as before, a black plywood floor was installed in the gallery. Each of the three exhibitions of Guyton's black paintings, held in New York, Frankfurt, and Paris in 2007 and 2008, was a show of ten paintings structured around this type of floor. The black floor, which was itself a reference to that in his studio at the time, created a chromatic and mnemonic continuity between the floor and the ten paintings reflected in it.

If the production process was identical, however, the technology used was updated: the Epson professional printer was replaced by a more recent model, which resulted

in a change in the texture of the ink.[1] As in the earlier
exhibition, the TIFF file—a rectangle measuring 40 × 90
inches in black (the default color in Photoshop)—was
printed once or several times on canvases folded in half.
Using views of the 2008 show, Guyton endeavored to
reconstruct the original exhibition layout precisely, and
then asked a photographer to produce a new set of photographs taken from the same angles. The sober-looking
invitation card featured the name of the artist, followed by
the title of the exhibition, which was simply the dates of
the previous show: *26 avril–7 juin 2008*.

Through this apparently self-reflexive gesture—an
exhibition speaking of itself in the past—the artist seems to
challenge conventional assumptions regarding the gallery
show as a demonstration of original creative prowess. Often
the aim is to produce new pieces, or to generate a new set
of relationships between works that make it possible to track
the progress of an artist's career, accompanied by critical
commentary over the ensuing months. Many artists end up
inflecting their exhibitions by making tiny variations, like
a repeated trick; here, Guyton seeks the exact opposite:
"[The first time] it was about bringing the studio into the
gallery. And in this situation I feel like the repetition of
the exhibition is in a way solidifying or objectifying the first
exhibition."[2]

At first one might think that the attempt at "objecti-
fication" simply enables people to remember the exhibition,
even those who have only seen pictures of it: in a way, to
materialize a memory. This sense of an afterimage would
have the effect of highlighting the singularity of the gallery
space and the context it brings with it. But Guyton adds:
"The first exhibition was very connected to the building and
the gallery space. The second time, it emerges from the
space again, or it penetrates the space again. I feel there's
a similarity with a record and a sound, a time that is *engraved*
into the space." The viewer might thus consider the exhibition as a whole as inseparable from the previous show,
lending yet more attention to the specific context of the
gallery. Even if the paintings in the second show seem
"engraved" in the wall, what is involved at the same time is
the remembered images that make the pictures in the second
show almost immaterial, tending to disturb the traditional

"old-fashioned real experience" of the reception of painting, as Guyton ironically puts it. Since the exhibition itself is the central proposition here, viewers adopt a different vantage point for the current show: one that is on a different level, or needs to be. "This time, the photos we took of the exhibition, the memory of the exhibition, and the exhibition itself become templates that can be reprinted, reactivated, reperformed [...] So [it is] a return to that exhibition as a file." The file is, moreover, now located in the cloud, as Guyton states in the press release. In 2008, the paintings made reference to the site of their production via the reconstruction of Guyton's studio floor in the gallery, but in 2014 this is no longer the case; he has since moved to a new studio. The exhibition does not refer to anything but the memory of itself.

It makes a certain sense that one might have the strange impression of having seen this exhibition before, and hence may experience a sensation of déjà vu, since the exhibition exists both as a set of images "rematerialized" at a precise moment, and as a series of images circulating on the Internet, whether as exhibition views from 2008 or from 2014. Visitors are thus not only confronted with the exhibition on view in the gallery, but also with their memories of the first show (if they saw it), and photographs or online images of either one of the two exhibitions.

Psychologists refer to déjà vu as an illusory repetition, a form of false recognition. As Paolo Virno puts it, déjà vu could also be seen as a new contemporary pathology of memory, whose symptoms resurface in the way experience and its representation seem nearly to coincide,[3] as we currently observe on social networks such as Instagram, Facebook, and Twitter. Contemporary art is subject to these unsettling mnemonic repetitions, especially when views of a show circulate online just before or during a show's opening. The viewer is submitted to continuous flows of representation without the bodily, articulated experience of memory. Perhaps we have even reached a point where representations no longer correspond to their referent in the present. For example, as Hito Steyerl points out, photographs taken on smartphones are tweaked using algorithms designed to reconstitute new images based on the preceding ones, so we actually only perceive the present via images of the past.[4] In such a situation, these images no longer correspond to the indexical representation of a film camera. The viewer has the disconcerting feeling of having experienced something before—albeit in another manner.

Let us now imagine what it would be like to see the exhibition for the first time without having seen the previous show, whether in person or via installation views. In the press release, Guyton stresses the sensory aspects of the exhibition: "The density has increased. Condensed into a single work. The noise is louder." He might be equating the thick texture of the ink with that of "noise." The metaphor of sound is also apparent in his description of the way the exhibition was produced: "Like the idea of sound engraved into a record, or that over time the work could be formed through pressure." The metaphor of the vinyl record—an analog, mechanical recording—contrasts sharply with that of digital technology, although the latter is the source of his paintings. But Guyton adds: "I was actually making a comparison to geologic formations of rock." He considers the gallery walls as a support for the paintings in the same way a vinyl record is a support for sound; and he draws a parallel between the production of the paintings and the process by which metamorphic rock is formed, through pressure or temperature altering the rock's texture and even its chemical composition. (It is notable that, at his retrospective at the Whitney Museum, Guyton also presented two photographs of a cave in which different rock strata were exposed.[5]) It is, thus, no longer the layers of matter that are used to talk about texture, but instead the transformation of matter itself. Six years after the first show, this new series is presented more as a transformation, one that is analogous to the workings of memory. The exhibition thus functions as a temporal pictorial apparatus, in which memory operates not only on the level of information—as a set of data to download—but also on a material level.

David Joselit argues that the field of painting seems to be getting closer and closer to time-based practices, in that its function, too, is becoming transitive.[6] It involves moving an image from one site or one time to another. Here, for

Guyton, it also involves transporting a painting from one moment to another, from one exhibition to another, yet in the same location, amplifying the déjà-vu effect. But there is another level of déjà vu that provokes a misunderstanding in the current American reception of his work. The exhibition may spark a memory of the 2008 show, or its photographic documentation, but that itself activates recognition of other things we believe we have already seen: exhibition views showing black monochromes—or, say, the near-monochromes of the New York School—in the white cube of a gallery or museum space. Such works are among the most obvious archetypes of modernism in painting.

This is not the first time Guyton has put into circulation some forms associated with the art of the 1960s and 1970s by manipulating the processes by which we remember. In 2003, using photographs and drawing from his memory, he made a plywood reconstruction of a minimalist sculpture that he used to walk by every day in Manhattan before it was exiled to the suburbs.[7] It was the negative image of this sculpture and what it represents as a form in the history of art, that came to interest him the most. With the Continuous Project collective, he later gave a new lease of life to the Dia Art Foundation archives from the early 1990s with performances based on transcriptions of symposia or "bootlegs" of texts. His recycling of discursive material relating to the critical reception of art is also evident in the *Black Paintings* catalogue, where he reprints three versions of a text on the black paintings by John Kelsey in each of the languages of the countries where the shows took place.[8] The catalogue reflects Guyton's repeated, deliberately laborious attempts to print a high-quality image using laser-printing methods. The text is treated in the same way as the images of the exhibition views, printed again when illegible because of the imperfections in the printing process, creating an effect akin to a productive stammer. For Guyton, an artwork is shaped by different language structures, either mechanical or human. In contrast to the earlier exhibition, described as the result of the articulation of different mechanical or digital languages (files/printer/canvases), the current show implies an indexical relation to discourse, which is also why the text of the press release plays such an important role.

Playing with misunderstandings and responding to them by staying one step ahead is an integral part of art making. We might only have seen in the doubling of this exhibition another predictable stage in the cat-and-mouse game with the market, a riposte that involves running away to a meta-level or using stubborn repetition as a response to the accelerated circulation of images on the Web. But Guyton gives things a different twist in the Paris gallery: the visual information that constitutes the show is as if *engraved* in the walls, which thus themselves act as a support.

In 2014, the process of reception has changed; it is noisier, we are confronted with more information: critical, historical, and sociological information online; different sorts of memories (including "false" memories); as well as the kind of sensory experience that has become more and more difficult to achieve. Painting only exists within a web of relations to preceding or subsequent images. Virno indicates that this crisis of perception could be overcome by means of language, which would allow us to articulate memories and to historicize the present, but Guyton proposes another solution here, whereby painting speaks of itself and its exhibition context as a materialized memory of the past and the present—whichever it may be.

[1] The new model that replaced the Epson Stylus Pro 9600 UltraChrome was the Epson Stylus Pro 9900 UltraChrome, which uses the Vivid Magenta ink upgrade.

[2] This quote and those that follow—except where another source is cited—are from an unpublished interview with Wade Guyton by the author.

[3] Paolo Virno, *Déjà Vu and the End of History*, trans. David Broder, Verso, London/New York 2015, p. 55.

[4] Hito Steyerl, "Politics of Post-Representation: In Conversation with Marvin Jordan," *DIS*, 2014, http://dismagazine.com/disillusioned-2/62143/hito-steyerl-politics-of-post-representation/ (last accessed June 2017).

[5] *The Devil's Hole (left and right)*, 1999.

[6] David Joselit, "On Abstraction Then and Now," *Artforum*, vol. XLIX, no. 11, Summer 2011.

[7] Scott Rothkopf, "Operating System," *Wade Guyton OS*, exh. cat., Whitney Museum of Art, New York 2012, p. 14.

[8] John Kelsey, "100%," see this volume p. 108–115.

Reclaimed Zones: Guyton's Rooms
Bettina Funcke

View of the exhibition *Wade Guyton*, Kunsthalle Zürich, Zurich, 2013

During his travels through Italy in 1798, Johann Wolfgang von Goethe famously made note of a remarkable shift taking place in the very definition, practice, and perception of art: whereas artistic objects had traditionally been made locally and to order—with paintings and sculptures commissioned and understood as integral parts of the buildings for which they had been designed, structuring rituals while embodying hierarchies and histories within the court and church—more recently they displayed a novel kind of mobility. As Goethe remarked, surveying the artistic production of previous centuries, "[w]ith few exceptions, works of art remained generally in the same location for which they were made. However, now a great change has occurred that, in general as well as specifically, will have important consequences for art."[1] From our current vantage point, we can say that Goethe was articulating a change taking place with respect not only to art, but also to its broader context: artworks were no longer being created and regarded strictly as the private property of a church or aristocratic line, but instead were being conceived as objects intended for contemplation by a broader populace within a public realm. Indeed, the shift Goethe beheld was the very dawning of modernism, signifying the start not of any brief period style, but instead of an entire emergent epistemology: the invention of art history, art museums, and a new public sphere oriented around a sympathetic bourgeois audience. Goethe was articulating nothing less than an entirely new way for art to be seen and placed.

Put another way, art as we understand it today has only been around for some 200 years. And so it should perhaps come as no surprise that we should once again find ourselves in a moment of historical transition, facing remarkably similar questions and pressures with respect to art and its context. As we move from a physical to an increasingly digitized culture—and to an economy steeped in speculation—generations of artists are prompted to redefine the place of art, its material and modes of production, reception, and dissemination. If Goethe observed the passage of one age to another, so we may offer witness to how our contemporary sense of space, place, time, and movement in art and culture also becomes merely the stuff of memory.

Such a charged sense of transition resonates strongly with Wade Guyton's recent move from making individual paintings to seemingly site-specific installations—works that you might call "Guyton Rooms." As seen in a recent exhibition at Petzel Gallery in New York (2014), these new works are very much *in situ*: paintings made to fit rooms, define rooms, even become rooms of a kind. Such installations feel quiet, simple, and powerfully resolved. Yet such stability would seem, on its face, to be at odds with the ephemerality and elusiveness of our evolving digital culture and economies. As the Petzel exhibition is just one part of a year's worth of works made for specific spaces, both institutional and commercial—including the Kunsthalle Zürich, the Art Institute of Chicago, and Galerie Chantal Crousel in Paris—I want to think about these "Guyton Rooms" in relation to the history of placing art, asking how this artist's work might answer the following questions: Where does art live now? How are works seen and experienced? Who puts the pieces there and under what circumstances?

***

To engage with such questions, consider theorist Boris Groys' previous reflection on that historical moment when art moved from a patronage system to a museum system. As he observes, works at the time "were accessible and available as objects of contemplation. But they were not [yet] accessible and available as objects of purchase and sale. The classical museum is not allowed to sell its holdings. [Contemporary] art emerged out of this gesture of distancing with regard to the consumer context."[2] In other words, with the emergence of the museum came a new kind of aesthetic distancing of the art object from its beholder. But such distancing inevitably allowed for a second distancing in turn, as private collectors eventually joined the stage, with the result that artists found themselves caught between the protection of the museum and exposure to a new free market.

For his part, Guyton has always worked with contradictions, inserting his structures into larger systems and seeing how they respond to pressure. In this regard, one could say that his new Rooms are partly intended to respond to the changing art market, forcing questions of whether artists can control the parameters and meaning of their work—particularly when it becomes the focus of intense financial speculation in the economy of a vastly expanded art world. As Guyton explains, his new works are printed to fit their particular display spaces, which means that they are meticulously and laboriously installed over many days. Moreover, as the artist has said of his rooms, considering the black, wall-size canvases with which they began: "I did think I was letting the black paintings 'un-become' paintings, or express themselves more architecturally. Or let the building or the spaces determine where the paintings should end and relate to each other. And allow those pressures to give form to the work."[3] This aspect effectively slows the circulation of the works once they have been made, because rooms are much harder to collect than paintings. Indeed, the gesture itself is more difficult to grasp, introducing a pause when it comes to any impulse to collect: what are the implications of faithfully recreating a commercial gallery experience in toto within a domestic or institutional setting when one purchases such a room?

While prompting such questions is a form of artistic control, we must nevertheless take note of how Guyton is making his entire model subject to the terms of circulation. The work is now so specific that clients and patrons have difficulty replicating the rooms. Guyton must travel to potential sites to assess the locale, personally overseeing any installation, documentation, or de-installation. At times, a matching room simply cannot be built at this new location, and he must decide how to reconfigure the work for its new surroundings. But by virtue of how this modularity is now part of Guyton's work—in a sense, it *is* the work—it is the very sense of *locating* the art that is being transported. If the development of the installation form offered artists in previous times a way to respond to the dislocations of an emerging marketplace—as was the case for the Russian Constructivists and the French avant-garde—it must be acknowledged that curatorial and art historical practice soon followed suit. Art was eventually understood not merely as a thing, but as a space and set of spatial relationships. And when making rooms, Guyton necessarily engages with this altered (or distanced, if you will) sense of location.

Guyton has always had a talent for engaging questions of space in his work, although this aspect of his practice has been largely overlooked due to the excitement generated by his painting. For example, much of his early, spatially-aware work was produced for specific, local, physical contexts: his precisely reassembled pile of found scrap wood placed upside down under a bridge in *Brewster, New York* (2002), or the room-filling platform produced as his Master's thesis work at Hunter College, which effectively presented viewers with a figure of participation cast as an alienating obstacle. Such pieces were influenced both by 1960s and 1970s ideas—of Minimalism, Conceptual art, and site-specificity—and by 1990s ideas about evolving social relations between viewer, space, and object. Guyton's *Drawing for Sculpture the Size of a House* (2001)—a photograph showing domestic architecture blacked out with ink—

might stand as a metaphor or emblem for this period, and as a harbinger of the artist's architecturally-determined work to come.

Guyton then moved to what would become his signature working style, which revolved around autonomous objects that were not tied to a specific locale: digitally printed canvases and "printer drawings," as well as "U" and chair sculptures. All these objects could circulate with ease, having been made to be owned; yet very quickly, and as important, Guyton underscored how they were to be moved and put into context. To explain the latter point, even as his pieces were being widely collected (or better, in response to that growing dynamic), the artist began once more to anchor the work in given spaces—placing sofas and chairs in relation to his paintings and displaying groups of his drawings in room-filling arrays of vitrines. He started importing the black, plywood floor of his studio into his exhibitions, claiming the very ground under viewers' feet for painting. These works could no longer be focused on as self-contained objects; they instead had to be considered as sets of works and gestures set in relationship with one another. Gradually, Guyton was forcing another sort of reception.

By extension, his most recent installations encompass the built architecture as a whole, yet the spatial dialogue among rooms is equally important as the interaction between paintings, or between paintings and sculptures, or paintings and furniture. In fact, in these most recent works it becomes unclear where the art begins or ends, or even how many pieces there are. Returning to the aforementioned Petzel exhibition, for instance, one could say that five paintings and a sculpture are on view; one could also say there are three separate pieces, because the rooms themselves have determined the fabrication parameters and constitute the artistic gesture, and there are, after all, three rooms. And would it not be important to consider not only the tension between the pairs of paintings in each room, but also the relationship between the two larger rooms and, in turn, how you move between them?

***

Such work conflates the site of production and reception, and thus is chiefly activated through very specific invitations and commissions to make in situ work. To consider the implications for this artist who works primarily in situ, it might then be helpful to examine the work of two older practitioners of the form—artists who may initially seem to have little to do with one another, or with Guyton, but who arguably offer common ground and new insights for his work.

Taken at face value, John Knight would clearly seem to be a very different artist. Based on the West Coast, he belongs to an earlier generation, possessed by a deep personal grounding in Conceptual art and the beginnings of Institutional Critique. However, Benjamin H. D. Buchloh has underlined Knight's context-specific art as a polemical, forced collapse of the distinctions between sculpture, architecture, and design,[4] and this approach offers a remarkable precedent for what is happening in Guyton's work. Like Knight, Guyton engages the relationship between primary site and secondary site: in his case, moving from *in situ* to *ex situ*, which often means from exhibition to book design. In addition, both artists pit the language of art against the language of design—although, very significantly, Knight emphasizes design as the apparatus standing at the base of capitalist ideology while Guyton (even as he may acknowledge Knight's point) puts the history of design to *use*, just as he does the history of art, drawing on aesthetic malleability and formal inspiration. Here, "use" can be a simple gesture: taking something that is already there —a chair, the page of a book, a sofa, a painting, or a room— and adding to it, setting it against something else. Of course, the gesture must look easy, and it must look good; history must continue, even if it cannot be said to progress.

This distinction points to the most crucial difference between these two artists, which lies in their attitudes toward resistance: while they may share thematic strategies and interests, Knight's oeuvre and temperament are marked by explicit resistance, whether to the market, the art object, or the politics around art; whether to a wrong comment, inadequate writing, or all the tendencies of the rotten times we live in. Over the past four decades, Knight has maintained a high level of resistance to commercialization, making only selective engagements with institutions, and usually the in situ nature of his work carries an implicit critique. He stands for a refusal to compromise, and for a certain withdrawal. By contrast, Guyton displays a relative ease and openness that allows him to engage with many of art making's contradictions, setting the provocative simplicity of digitally-produced work against its complex physical needs, and the anonymous logic of code against the spatial-sensual manifestation of painting. In the process, he proposes links between design, capital, and technology that are quite similar to those emphasized in Knight's work, but only while embracing many of the art world's forms and forums. The generational difference has presented each artist with a specific set of options and limits, in other words, and Guyton may feel that he no longer has the option to take a purist position. As Buchloh has pointed out, formerly radical sculptural and spatial paradigms now represent "conditions of spatial domination and perceptual control against which any radical sculptural practice in the present inevitably would have to position itself."[5] In this respect, Guyton is a participant—perhaps we all are, and this paradox is precisely what leads him to pursue his recent formal strategies: How to be a participant and yet continue to challenge the relationships between art, architecture, technology, design, and site?

When he first arrived in New York, Guyton was extensively exposed to material forms and spatial relations that may shed light on the particular tensions within his work, and, more specifically, on some of his artistic choices and interests. Beginning in the mid-1990s and for nearly ten years, he was employed as a guard at the Dia Art Foundation in New York, where he was strongly affected by its ethos and its artists. In Dia's carefully considered former spaces— which were imbued with such a determinedly quiet and slow and refined institutional culture—it was often hard for a viewer to know whether a given piece had been produced for the space or preexisting work had been so thoughtfully arranged that art and space merged into one. Thanks to Dia's commitment to year-long exhibitions, Guyton was able to experience such works in-depth, for many hours every day, and in this environment he began to consider all the ways an artwork might be related to space, time, and the movement of the viewer.

Significantly, during this period Richard Serra exhibited his *Torqued Ellipses* at the museum. In an interview for that show's catalogue, Serra speaks about his interest in the "ways of relating movement to material space [...] to think about sculpture in an open and extended field, in a way that is precluded when dealing with sculpture as an autonomous object." And then he goes on to say, echoing Dia's philosophy in a manner that is especially resonant with Guyton's recent work: "I found very important the idea of the body passing through space, and the body's movement not being predicated totally on image or sight or optical awareness, but on physical awareness in relation to space, place, time, movement."[6]

Like Knight, Serra has mainly made his work for institutions and public spaces, but he has also always made gallery shows, and does not seem to have any issues working with some of the most commercially powerful galleries. In fact, Serra needs them to support his projects, because over the course of his investigation of the relationship between site, work, and viewer, the work has developed uniquely stringent demands: larger spaces, reinforced floors, extra high ceilings, custom wall openings to import the sculptures, and so on. This is in situ artwork, to be sure, but the terms only allow for certain sites. The work does not simply respond to specific architectural or outdoor spaces, but tends to dominate, control, or redefine the situation, for better or for worse. As with Guyton's recent work, Serra's sculptures are explicitly made for commercial contexts, but they acknowledge implicitly that the terms for such contexts have changed—he pushes against their limits, making them more concrete—if you buy the piece you are going to have to set up a very special place to show it.

The pressures on Guyton's work—and possibly on that of his entire generation—are of course quite different than those that may have initially pushed Serra to explore similar ideas. In Guyton's case, it may well be a very contemporary loss of control having to do with digital abstraction that has provoked a new level of specific engagement with the physical, material details of the work—or more precisely, with the mutability of such physical, material details. In other words, it is possible that we are living through a watershed moment in art comparable to the earlier transition observed by Goethe. This may be a crude, early stage—a digital "Stone Age" of flaws and complexity—but we do know that we are redefining all forms of production, reproduction, communication, and dissemination, leading to deep structural shifts in the practice, perception, and place of art. Certainly, in culture at large, a belief in progress has been replaced by flexibility with uncertainty. Philosopher Zygmunt Baumann, for instance, suggests that this shift reflects a culture of digital "liquidity," in which the emphasis on art's autonomy has changed: "If in its 'solid' phase the heart of modernity was in controlling and fixing the future … under conditions of liquidity anything could happen yet nothing can be done with confidence and certainty."[7] A century ago, to be "modern" meant progress and the pursuit of some final state of perfection. Now it means infinite minor changes, with no final state in sight, and perhaps none desired. As the artist Seth Price, a close colleague of Guyton's, recently put it: "It was a deep irony that the mechanisms of digital culture were built on a binary fundament even as that culture sought to eradicate all opposition, contradiction, and friction on an ontological level, steadily reducing human variety to a kind of affirmative mush."[8]

In this situation, all artists and intellectuals thus face the question of how to regain a sense of control over what one is making, who it might be for, and where it goes. The early 21st century has presented installation-based artwork with striking difficulties, including not only the ever-expanding art market and its overproduction of consumer objects, but also a loss of control over material reality. To cite Buchloh once more: "[W]hatever spatial relations and material forms one might still experience outside of the … spectacularized spaces of control, and electronic digitization, they now appear merely as abandoned zones, as residual objects and leftover spaces, rather than as elementary givens from which new spatial parameters and new object relations could be configured in sculptural terms in the present."[9]

In a way, Guyton's new work points to the tensions of these abandoned zones, for it merges "abandoned" computational space and "wasted" physical space. At Petzel, these abandoned zones and elementary givens were the focus of the exhibition: three bare rooms, canvas, the colors black and white. What we look at and walk through was produced with a digital file and an Epson 11880 printer, yet the project was also made through the complex physical interactions of handling and placing. Each work was printed on folded, extra-long rolls of Belgian linen; each displays two black rectangles printed in such a way that they are not quite lined up, before extending to a sort of "left-over" area of off-white fabric surface, which is marked with the gray streaks and faint lines that result from having been pulled through Guyton's printer.

Walking through the "Guyton Rooms" opens up a further understanding of their particular tensions. The artist's canvas works are usually hung vertically, but here are put forward as horizontals, in effect measuring the architectural space from corner to corner. The works are installed in pairs, one pair to a room, and each pair marks a space within the architecture that differs from the containment of the architecture. Each pair reclaims the space by making it palpable, demarcating its limits and parameters. The installation brings the two main gallery rooms into a curious relationship, again dependent on one's movement within the space: The room in the back is framed by two wall-filling canvas pieces that meet in a corner; and the preceding, narrower room is defined by two wall-length works facing off against one another. Walking through the gallery, one experiences the rooms' spatial relations—their volumes, the differing ceiling heights, the movements of the canvas pairs, the changing light, the concrete floor and its small shifts in tone. When one enters the spaces held by these black-and-white planar pairs, one's body registers the simultaneous compression and extension of the space; one is pulled into the rooms and then immediately and subtly pushed out again. The surrounding walls seem to exude pressure: the black absorbs the light, the white areas reflect the light, and the space's physicality shifts as one moves within it. All this recalls something Serra said: "[Y]our vision is peripatetic and not reduced to framing an image. It includes and is dependent upon memory and anticipation … The relationship of time, space, walking, and looking."[10]

Guyton's Rooms at Petzel quietly hold in suspension the tension between the digital and physical. In a simple gesture they freeze the historical moment in which we find ourselves, a point of paradigmatic transition. On the one hand are the digital files and the robotic printing machines that are fed linen and which, with a push of a button, spit out the coveted canvases. (When I recently saw the large Epson printers rolled into a corner of Guyton's studio, they looked a bit weary, but forever hungry to produce.) On the other hand, we have the familiar, old-fashioned, slow, physical world, with its laws and limits as to size, weight, movement, light, gravity, humidity, and the endless potential for perfection and tweaking that defines art in situ.

These contradictory components contribute to the work's particular energy, which has to do with desire and scale: a balance between attraction and repulsion, an invitation and an unyielding force, abstraction and figuration. And figuration here means a viewer's bodily awareness as well as the act of giving figure to the abstraction of digital production itself. This is what is haunting about the "Guyton Rooms." They offer a corporeal experience of this new cultural condition of digital abstraction and digital liquidity, even as we live in a physical world defined by the perspective of one person in one place at one time.

[1] Johann Wolfgang von Goethe, introduction to his *Propyläen, Goethes sämtliche Werke*, vol. 5, Tétotes Frères, Paris 1836, p. 486

[2] Boris Groys, "What Is Art?/Everyone Has to Be an Artist/After the End of Mass Culture/Egypt as Quick Run," in *The Future of Art: A Manual*, ed. Ingo Nierman, Sternberg Press, Berlin 2011, p. 219–237.

[3] Guyton in an email to the author, July 24, 2014.

[4] See Benjamin H. D. Buchloh, "Knight's Negations," in *John Knight: October Files 16*, ed. André Rottmann, MIT Press, Cambridge, Massachusetts 2014, p. 161.

[5] Buchloh, "Knight's Negations," p. 159–160.

[6] Richard Serra, "Interview with Richard Serra by Lynne Cooke and Michael Govan," in *Richard Serra: Torqued Ellipses*, Dia Center for the Arts, New York 1997, p. 27–28.

[7] Zygmunt Baumann, *Liquid Modernity*, Polity, Cambridge 2012, p. x, xiv.

[8] Seth Price, *Fuck Seth Price*, Leopard, New York 2015, p. 21.

[9] Buchloh, "Knight's Negations," p. 160.

[10] Serra, "Interview with Richard Serra by Lynne Cooke and Michael Govan," p. 28–29.

Imprint

EDITORS
Tim Griffin, Clément Dirié

WRITERS
Daniel Baumann, Kirsty Bell, Boško Blagojević &
Sam Pulitzer, Johanna Burton, Catherine Chevalier,
Holland Cotter, Bettina Funcke, Tim Griffin, Achim
Hochdörfer, John Kelsey, Scott Rothkopf, Vincent Pécoil,
Peter Schjeldahl

EDITORIAL COORDINATION
Clément Dirié, with the collaboration of
Barbara Biedermann

COPY EDITING AND PROOFREADING
Clare Manchester

DESIGN CONCEPT
Gavillet & Rust, Geneva

DESIGN
Nicolas Eigenheer, Nicolas Leuba

PRINT AND BINDING
Musumeci S.p.A., Quart (Aosta)

TYPEFACE
Genath (www.optimo.ch)

PHOTO CREDITS
Stefan Altenburger: 146; Ron Amstutz: 4, 26, 46, 116, 132;
Martin Argyroglo: 108; Wade Guyton: 30, 40; Florian
Kleinefenn: 138; Lamay Photo: 86; Thomas Mueller: 90;
Courtesy of Wade Guyton: 36, 76, 122; Courtesy of the
Kunsthalle Zürich: 66

All works are courtesy of the artist. All texts are reproduced
with the kind authorization of the writers. We would like
to thank them for their collaboration.

© 2018, the artist, the photographers, and JRP | Ringier
Kunstverlag AG
© From the *New York Times*, December 14, 2007. 2018,
The New York Times. All rights reserved. Used by permission
and protected by the Copyright Laws of the United States.
The printing, copying, redistribution, or retransmission of
this content without express permission is prohibited.

All rights reserved. No part of this publication may be
reproduced, stored in a retrieval system, or transmitted,
in any form, or by any means, electronic, mechanical,
or otherwise without prior permission in writing from the
publisher.

This book is published with the Kunsthalle Zürich, Zurich.

PUBLISHED BY
JRP | Ringier
Limmatstrasse 270
CH–8005 Zurich
T +41 43 311 27 50
E info@jrp-ringier.com
www.jrp-ringier.com

IN CO-EDITION WITH
Les presses du réel
35, rue Colson
F–21000 Dijon
T +33 3 80 30 75 23
E info@lespressesdureel.com
www.lespressesdureel.com

ISBN 978-3-03764-473-7 (JRP | Ringier)
ISBN 978-2-84066-945-6 (Les presses du réel)

Distribution

JRP | Ringier publications are available internationally
at selected bookstores and from the following distribution
partners:

GERMANY AND AUSTRIA
Vice Versa Distribution
www.viceversaartbooks.com

FRANCE
Les presses du réel
www.lespressesdureel.com

SWITZERLAND
AVA Verlagsauslieferung AG
www.ava.ch

UK AND OTHER EUROPEAN COUNTRIES
Cornerhouse Publications HOME
www.cornerhousepublications.org

USA, CANADA, ASIA, AND AUSTRALIA
ARTBOOK | D. A. P.
www.artbook.com

For a list of our partner bookshops or for any general
questions, please contact JRP | Ringier directly at
info@jrp-ringier.com, or visit our homepage
www.jrp-ringier.com for further information.

Documents Series 25:
Tim Griffin [ed.]
Writings on Wade Guyton

This book is the twenty-fifth
volume in the "Documents" series,
dedicated to critics' writings.

The series was founded by
Lionel Bovier and Xavier Douroux.

This volume is dedicated to
the memory of Xavier Douroux
who passed away in June 2017.
Co-founder of the art center
Le Consortium (Dijon) where Wade
Guyton exhibited in 2016, and of
the publishing house Les presses
du réel, Xavier Douroux was a true
visionary and a tireless missionary
for the arts and the life of ideas.

Also available

DOCUMENTS SERIES (IN ENGLISH)

John Baldessari, *More Than You Wanted to Know
About John Baldessari*
ISBN 978-3-03764-192-7 (JRP | Ringier) [*Vol. 1*]
ISBN 978-3-03764-256-6 (JRP | Ringier) [*Vol. 2*]

Sarah Burkhalter & Laurence Schmidlin, *Spacescapes.
Dance & Drawing since 1962*
ISBN 978-3-03764-469-0 (JRP | Ringier)
ISBN 978-2-84066-917-3 (Les presses du réel)

Joshua Decter, *Art Is a Problem*
ISBN 978-3-03764-195-8 (JRP | Ringier)
ISBN 978-2-84066-621-9 (Les presses du réel)

Gabriele Detterer & Maurizio Nannucci, *Artist-Run Spaces*
ISBN 978-3-03764-191-0 (JRP | Ringier)
ISBN 978-2-84066-512-0 (Les presses du réel)

Christian Höller, *Time Action Vision*
ISBN 978-3-03764-124-8 (JRP | Ringier)
ISBN 978-2-84066-396-6 (Les presses du réel)

Hans Ulrich Obrist, *A Brief History of Curating*
ISBN 978-3-905829-55-6 (JRP | Ringier)
ISBN 978-2-84066-287-7 (Les presses du réel)

Hans Ulrich Obrist, *A Brief History of New Music*
ISBN 978-3-905829-190-3 (JRP | Ringier)
ISBN 978-2-84066-619-6 (Les presses du réel)

Igor Zabel, *Contemporary Art Theory*
ISBN 978-3-03764-238-2 (JRP | Ringier)
ISBN 978-2-84066-573-1 (Les presses du réel)